48

D1785092

# Cooking Today Eating Tomorrow

## by
## Jan Hopcraft

WARD LOCK LIMITED · LONDON

For everyone who has helped to eat the way
through this book

© Jan Hopcraft 1972

ISBN 0 7063 1007 1

This edition published in Great Britain in 1973
by Ward Lock Limited, 116 Baker Street, London,
W1M 2BB

First published by Methuen & Co. Ltd.

Printed and bound by Cox & Wyman Ltd.,
London, Fakenham and Reading

# Contents

**Dinner Party Menus**

*page* 8

    recipes specially chosen to ensure that the
cook has a drink with the guests before eating,
no menu includes more than one dish which has to
be made from start to finish on the day of entertaining;
designed for four to six people.

**Lunch Party Menus**

42

    though simpler, these follow the pattern of dinner
party menus and can be used as alternatives; they
also serve four to six people.

**Fork Supper Menus**

68

    hot dishes for winter entertaining and cold
food for summer evening or after-theatre parties;
the quantities given feed ten, twelve or sixteen
people.

**Menus for the Unexpected Guest**

86

    dishes made from foods available in the store
cupboard.

# Contents

**Ideas for Drinks Parties** *page* 98
    pâté, dips and canapés.

**Vegetables** 109

**Sauces** 122

**Miscellaneous** 132

    *Measurement Equivalents, Metric and USA* 139
    *Oven Temperature Chart* 139
    *Culinary Terms* 140
    *Index* 141

**Important:** *The spoon quantities given in this book are based on plastic measuring spoons. Level spoons have been used throughout unless otherwise stated.*

# Introduction

When I first came to London I lived in a minute bed-sitting room at the top of a house in Knightsbridge. It was so small that three guests were the maximum, they sat in a row on the bed, I sat opposite, and the empty plates from each course went straight out of the window to join the herbs in my window-box. Luckily, although the plants suffered, the box never collapsed on to the heads of the passers-by. This taught me one of the fundamental rules for entertaining – the importance of being well organized in advance. When the door bell rings and the guests arrive, it is no fun to be caught with a hot, shiny face and so, on the following pages, I have provided a collection of menus to ensure that the guests are not the only ones to sit down with a drink before eating.

The menus are for lunch, dinner, and fork supper parties, and there are ideas, too, for eats to go with drinks, and recipes for tinned and other store-cupboard foods to feed the unexpected guest. Most of the menus can be prepared in advance, and none includes more than one dish which has to be made from start to finish on the day itself. I have also attempted to give the preparation time for every recipe, but this should be treated only as a guide, to compare the merits of one dish with another. These menus are intended for busy people, including those who arrive home late wondering what possessed them to invite six people to dinner at eight. Entertaining should be fun and the hard work over before the guests arrive. In fact the single-handed hostess should be free of the strain that made Mrs Beeton refer to the pre-dinner gathering as 'the great ordeal'.

It would be wrong to pretend that one can have really good food all the time without effort. Some of the recipes in this book are quick and easy; others rely for their success on sauces and lengthy cooking, but are well worth the trouble providing the work is over before any guests appear.

Sometimes there are hurried days when shopping can be easier than cooking. And it is useful to remember that a little careful marketing at a delicatessen and a greengrocer can provide the occasional feast without any work. The Londoner has Soho to choose from, and an expedition to this area should be on the itinerary of every London visitor who is even remotely interested in food. Lina Stores in Brewer Street makes a good place to start; they provide delicious Italian bread, pasta of every kind, large black olives, mozzarella cheese and cold meats like milanese salami and mortadella. Across the road at Richards, you can see octopi lying in a black ink bed of their own making, or buy fresh sardines, which are delicious dusted with flour, fried in butter and served with slices of lemon and fresh, crusty bread. Carry on to Rupert Street where you will find lettuces of every variety, chinese cabbage, watercress, strawberries, grapes and melons. Back in Brewer Street walk on to Hamburger, to buy smoked cod's roe paste or smoked salmon paste. Both are ready to eat accompanied by toast, butter, a squeeze of lemon juice and a few black olives. Hamburger are also well known for their buckling, smoked sturgeon and kippers. On to Camisa in Old Compton Street for pine nuts, dried breadcrumbs and inexpensive French olive oil. Opposite, at Del Monico, you will find wines at every price and a queue right down the street at Christmas time. The subject of wine, however, I leave to the experts except to say that a well chosen *vin ordinaire* makes a pleasant accompaniment to any meal. Presentation counts as much with wine as with food. By decanting a simple wine you may prevent it being pre-judged by its label.

# Dinner Party Menus

# Dinner Party Menus

*(serve 6 except where indicated)*

| | | |
|---|---|---|
| Egg and Liver Pâté | *pages* | 10–11 |
| Cod Coulibiac | | |
| Ginger Cream | | |
| | | |
| Squid Soup | *(Serves* 4) | 12–13 |
| Roast Pheasant with Raisins and Whisky | | |
| Mousse d'Amandes au Caramel Glacée | | |
| | | |
| Cream of Watercress Soup | | 14–15 |
| Jugged Hare | | |
| Crème Brûlée | | |
| | | |
| Mussels with Garlic Breadcrumbs | | 16–17 |
| Stuffed Shoulder of Lamb | *(Serves* 4) | |
| Vanilla Ice-cream with Chocolate Sauce | | |
| | | |
| Baked Avocado Pears with Crab Meat | *(Serves* 4) | 18–19 |
| Coq au Vin | | |
| Orange Cream Soufflé Surprise | | |
| | | |
| Artichokes with Garlic Breadcrumbs | | 20–21 |
| Vitello Tonnato | | |
| Brandy Snaps | | |
| | | |
| Crab Mousse | | 22–23 |
| Baked Gammon with Prunes and Apricots | | |
| Lemon Meringues | | |

Egg Mousse                                              *pages* 24–25
Paupiettes de Porc
Melon Baskets

Cold Mackerel with Mayonnaise                                  26–27
Pigeon Casserole
Oeufs à la Neige

Fish Pâté                                  (*Serves* 4)           28–29
Duck Casserole with Oranges and Cider
Chocolate Pots

Cod with Crab Sauce Mornay                                     30–31
Pork Chops with Anchovies
Blackcurrant Ice-cream

Barbecue Ribs with Sweet Spiced Sauce                          32–33
Stuffed Peppers
Profiteroles au Chocolat

Kipper Pâté                                                    34–35
Stuffed Courgettes, Aubergines and Tomatoes
Raisins avec Crème Chantilly

Cold Consommé with Mock Caviar and Soured Cream (*Serves* 4)   36–37
Fried Chicken
Hatch House Summer Pudding

Buckling Pâté                                                  38–39
Boeuf en Croûte
Caramel Oranges

Consommé Mousse                            (*Serves* 12)         40–41
Roast Turkey
Christmas Pudding

## Egg and Liver Pâté

*Can be made 1 day ahead    Action and cooking time 15 minutes*

½ lb chicken livers
3 tablespoons chopped onion
2 hard-boiled eggs, chopped
2 ozs butter
freshly ground pepper
salt

## Cod Coulibiac

*Can be prepared 1 day ahead    Action time 40 minutes    Cooking time 20–25 minutes*

4 cod steaks (about 1½ lbs)
½ lb puff pastry page 133*
4 ozs cooked rice**
½ lb mushrooms finely sliced
3 hard-boiled eggs, chopped
4 ozs butter
2 rashers chopped bacon

1 small onion finely chopped
parsley finely chopped
¼ teaspoon allspice
pinch of mace
pinch of nutmeg
salt and freshly ground pepper
1 egg lightly beaten – for brushing pastry

*Frozen pastry can be used.
**Cook the rice in beef consommé (about 10½ oz tin) and a ¼–½ as much water again.

## Ginger Cream

*Can be made 1 day ahead    Action time 10 minutes    No cooking*

½ pint (1¼ cups U.S.) double cream
4 tablespoons whisky
2 tablespoons stem ginger syrup
2 tablespoons castor sugar
2 egg whites
½ teaspoon powdered ginger
3 pieces stem ginger (decoration)

**Method.** Melt half the butter in a saucepan and fry the onion gently for 5 minutes. Add the chicken livers and cook them for about 6 or 7 minutes. Transfer the contents of the saucepan to a liquidizer. Add the rest of the butter cut in small pieces, the chopped egg, salt and freshly ground pepper and blend thoroughly. Pour into a pâté jar or individual ramekins and serve with toast and butter. This pâté is not as rich as the recipes given on pages 76 and 101.

**Method.** Melt half the butter in a frying pan and sauté the onion until it is transparent. Add the sliced mushrooms, chopped bacon, parsley, allspice, mace, nutmeg, salt, pepper and 1 tablespoon of water and cook until the mushrooms are soft; this will take about 5–10 minutes. Place the cod steaks in the pan and cook them for 2–3 minutes each side. Remove the pan from the fire, take out the cod steaks and put the mushroom mixture in a bowl to cool. Remove the skin and bones from the fish and keep these on one side if you plan to make a white wine sauce. Cut the fish into mouth-sized pieces. At this point the ingredients can be cooled and stored until the next day in covered containers in the refrigerator. An hour or two before cooking roll out the pastry in the shape of a rectangle about 14 in. by 16 in. Place half the rice in a layer down the centre, sprinkle over half the chopped egg, then half the mushroom mixture, then all the fish followed by the remains of the mushroom mixture, egg and lastly rice. Damp the edges of the pastry and draw the sides together pressing firmly. Brush the surface of the pastry with egg and cook for 20–25 minutes in a pre-heated 'very hot' oven (450F Mark 8); plan to start cooking 10 minutes before your guests sit down to eat the first course. Just before serving melt the rest of the butter and make a slit in the top of the coulibiac; pour the butter through the slit. White wine sauce, though not essential, goes well with this dish, see page 126.

**Method.** Place the whisky, ginger syrup, powdered ginger, castor sugar and cream in a bowl and whisk with an egg beater until thick. In another bowl whisk the egg whites until stiff. Fold the egg whites into the ginger mixture, spoon into individual glass bowls and chill. Decorate with small pieces of chopped stem ginger.

## Squid Soup

*Can be made 1 day ahead    Action time 30 minutes    Cooking time 30 minutes*

$\frac{3}{4}$ lb squid

3 tablespoons white wine

2 tablespoons olive oil

1$\frac{1}{4}$ pints (3$\frac{1}{8}$ cups U.S.) milk

1 rounded tablespoon flour

$\frac{1}{4}$ teaspoon salt

1 teaspoon paprika

1 medium sized onion finely chopped

freshly ground pepper

## Roast Pheasant with Raisins and Whisky

*Stuffing should be prepared in advance and the gravy can be prepared at the same time
Action time 20 minutes    Cooking time about 1 hour*

1 pheasant

6 rashers rindless bacon

2 slices crustless bread

2 ozs butter

watercress (optional garnish)

*Stuffing*

2 ozs raisins

1 packet Philadelphia cream cheese
(about 3 ozs)

2 tablespoons whisky

Simple gravy, page 125

Pheasant is traditionally accompanied by game chips, brussels sprouts, bread sauce, page 126, breadcrumbs, page 135 and gravy. Since game ships and brussels sprouts do not keep hot satisfactorily, try serving mashed potatoes and red cabbage instead.

## Mousse d'Amandes au Caramel Glacée

(CARAMEL ICE-CREAM)

*Make 1 day ahead    Action time 30 minutes    No cooking except for caramel*

4 eggs

2 tablespoons golden syrup

$\frac{1}{2}$ pint (1$\frac{1}{4}$ cups U.S.) double cream

*Caramel*

4 tablespoons castor sugar

4 tablespoons water

2 ozs almonds finely chopped – blanch first to remove skin

**Method.** Clean the squid by pulling off the head and cutting off the tentacles. Remove the skin from the bag-like part of the fish. Turn the bag-like part inside out and remove any remaining intestines and the transparent spine bone. Wash the squid thoroughly under running water and cut into small pieces. Heat the oil in a saucepan and gently fry the onion until transparent. Put the flour, paprika, salt and pepper in the pan and cook for 1 to 2 minutes before adding the body and the tentacles of the squid and cooking for a few more minutes. Remove from the stove and blend in the milk. Return to the fire and simmer for a few minutes before adding the wine; simmer gently for a further 20 minutes. Pour the soup into a liquidizer, keeping some of the pieces of squid on one side, and blend thoroughly. Since pulverizing squid does not produce a smooth purée it is necessary to sieve this soup. Reheat and add the pieces of squid before serving.

**Method.** *Stuffing:* Mix the whisky, cream cheese and raisins together and leave to stand for 24 hours. *Roast Pheasant:* Stuff the pheasant with the raisin mixture and cover the breast and legs with butter and bacon rashers. Toast the bread, cut each slice in two and sit the pheasant on these in a roasting pan. Pre-heat the oven to 'fairly hot' (400F Mark 6) and roast the pheasant on the centre shelf for about 50 minutes, basting from time to time. Remove the bacon and cook for a further 10 minutes to brown the pheasant's breast. Take out of the oven and sit the pheasant on a carving dish surrounded by the toast and watercress. The easiest timing is to put the bird in the oven 1 hour before the guests are due to sit down to dinner. While the first course is being eaten cover the bird with foil and keep it hot in a low oven. This will allow, if necessary, for 10–15 minutes additional cooking time. *Gravy:* Pour the surplus fat out of the pan in which the pheasant has been cooked. Place the simple gravy mixture in the pan and boil for 2 or 3 minutes.

**Method.** *Caramel:* first butter a piece of tinfoil approximately 12 in. square. Next put the sugar, water and almonds in a saucepan and boil until the syrup turns deep golden brown; remove from the fire and quickly pour on to the buttered tinfoil spreading the syrup out as far as possible. When it has set wrap the tinfoil over, fold the ends in, and hammer with a rolling pin to make caramel crumbs. *Ice-cream:* in separate bowls whip the egg whites until stiff and whip the cream. In a third bowl place the yolks, syrup and caramel crumbs and mix well together; gently fold in the cream and then the egg white. Finally put the mixture in a soufflé dish or an ice-cream tray and place in the freezing compartment of the refrigerator. For perfect smoothness, beat the ice-cream with a fork just before it hardens.

## Cream of Watercress Soup

*Can be made 1 day ahead    Action time 20 minutes    Cooking time 40 minutes*

1 pint (2½ cups U.S.) chicken stock
1 pint (2½ cups U.S.) milk
3 bunches watercress shredded finely
1 oz butter
1 onion finely chopped

4 tablespoons flour
¼ pint (⅝ cup U.S.) single cream
1 egg lightly beaten
salt and freshly ground pepper
6 small sprigs watercress for decoration

## Jugged Hare

*Can be made 1 day ahead    Action time 1¼ hours    Cooking time about 2 hours*

1 hare, jointed, plus the blood
1 large onion finely chopped
2 carrots sliced
2 sticks celery sliced
4 tablespoons port
1½ pints (3¾ cups U.S.) stock
1 tablespoon red currant jelly
2 ozs dripping
flour
beurre manié, see page 133

salt and freshly ground pepper
*Marinade*
4 tablespoons oil
4 tablespoons wine vinegar
1 tablespoon chopped onion
2 bay leaves
2 cloves garlic cut in 4 pieces
freshly ground pepper
Forcemeat rissoles page 136

## Crème Brûlée

*Make 1 day ahead    Action time 35 minutes    Cooking time about 1¼ hours*

1 pint (2½ cups U.S.) double cream
4 egg yolks
1 tablespoon castor sugar
2 drops vanilla essence
additional castor sugar for caramel

**Method.** Melt the butter and fry the onion slowly for 5 minutes; add the watercress and cook for a further 10 minutes with the lid on the pan. Take the lid off the pan and stir in the flour, cook for 1 or 2 minutes stirring all the time. Blend in the chicken stock and add salt and pepper; bring to the boil and simmer for 20 minutes before adding the milk and passing the soup through a sieve. **At this point the soup can be kept until the next day.** Pour it back into the pan and reheat, just before serving mix the cream with the egg and add to the soup; take great care that it does not boil.

**Method.** Put the hare pieces in one basin and the blood in another; mix the ingredients for the marinade together and pour them over the hare. Leave the hare sitting in the marinade for 3 hours or longer turning the pieces occasionally during that time. Wipe the meat and flour it. Melt the fat in a saucepan and brown the hare pieces for 3 to 4 minutes on each side. Put the hare in a warmed casserole and sauté the onion, celery and carrots for 5 to 6 minutes. Return the hare to the saucepan and add the marinade – from which the pieces of garlic should be removed – the stock, red currant jelly, salt and pepper. Bring the stock to boiling point and transfer the contents of the pan to a casserole. Place in a 'very cool' oven (250–275F Mark $\frac{1}{2}$–1) and simmer for $1\frac{1}{2}$–2 hours until the hare is tender. At the end of the cooking time, strain the stock into a saucepan, leaving the hare to keep warm in the casserole. Bring the stock to the boil and cook for 10 minutes to reduce the liquid. Lower the heat and add the port, the blood of the hare and, if necessary, a little beurre manié to further thicken the stock. Do not boil after the blood has been added, but simmer gently for 2 to 3 minutes. Pour the stock over the hare and add the forcemeat rissoles. Reheat in the oven or over a low flame. Serve with mashed potatoes and red cabbage, pages 118 and 114.

**Method.** Put the cream in a double saucepan or in a basin over simmering water and bring slowly to scalding point; this will take about 20 minutes. Meanwhile beat the yolks in a basin together with the sugar. Pour the scalded cream on to the yolks and stir well; add the vanilla essence. Return the mixture to the saucepan or basin and, stirring from time to time, slowly thicken over simmering water; this will take about 25 minutes. Pour the egg mixture into a shallow dish, set in a pan of boiling water and cook in a 'cool' oven (300F Mark 2) for 30 minutes. Remove from the pan and leave to stand overnight. A few hours before serving, cover the surface evenly with a thin layer of sugar. Place under a hot, pre-heated grill until the sugar caramelizes and becomes brown, this only takes about 2 minutes. Chill well before eating.

## Mussels with Garlic Breadcrumbs

*Action time 45 minutes    Cooking time 10 minutes*

4 pints mussels
1 small onion roughly chopped
1 bay leaf
½ pint (1¼ cups U.S.) cider
3 peppercorns
salt

*Garlic breadcrumbs:*
6 ozs butter
4 cloves garlic
5 tablespoons dried breadcrumbs
parsley finely chopped

Provide French bread to eat with this dish.

## Stuffed Shoulder of Lamb

*Can be prepared 1 day ahead    Action time 30 minutes*
*Cooking time about 2¼ hours*

1 boned shoulder (about 4½ lbs
    before boning)
2 cloves garlic
*Stuffing*
¾ lb sausage meat
1½ cups (1⅞ U.S.) breadcrumbs
1 onion finely chopped

2 ozs butter
1 egg lightly beaten
grated rind of 1 lemon
3 tablespoons chopped walnuts
1½ teaspoons oregano
salt and freshly ground pepper

## Vanilla Ice-cream with Chocolate Sauce

*Make ice-cream and sauce 1 day ahead    Action time 15 minutes    No cooking*
*except for sauce*

4 whites of egg
6 tablespoons castor sugar
½ pint (1¼ cups U.S.) double cream
2 drops vanilla essence
3 tablespoons chopped, burnt almonds for decoration, page 141
Chocolate sauce, pages 129, 130

Brandy Snaps

Christmas
Pudding

**Method.** For this dish you will have to leave your guests for about 10 minutes just before they sit down to dinner. *Mussels:* scrub and scrape mussel shells. To make sure that all the open mussels are alive, tap them with a knife and if they do not close up, discard; also throw away all mussels with broken or damaged shells. Place the onion, bay leaf, peppercorns and salt in a saucepan with the cider and boil for 3 minutes. Put the cleaned mussels in the boiling cider, the lid on the saucepan and steam for 5 minutes, shaking the saucepan from time to time. Remove the pan from the fire and drain the liquid from the mussels. Take away the empty shell from each mussel, and discard any which have not opened during the cooking. This is quick to do especially if you wear rubber gloves to prevent your fingers from getting burnt. Serve straight on to individual plates and cover with the garlic breadcrumbs. *Garlic breadcrumbs:* these can be prepared while the mussels are cooking. Melt the butter in a pan. Pound or squeeze the garlic cloves and place these together with the breadcrumbs in the pan with the butter. Gently fry for about 5 minutes and, just before using, add the chopped parsley. The mussels can, of course, be cleaned a few hours in advance.

**Method.** *Stuffing:* melt the butter in a pan and gently fry the onion for 5 minutes; add the sausage meat, walnuts, oregano, lemon rind, salt and pepper and cook for a further 10 minutes. Remove from the fire and stir in the breadcrumbs and then the egg. *Stuffed shoulder of lamb:* if stuffing the lamb the day before cooking, wait until the sausage mixture is completely cold before doing so. Trim off any excess fat from the lamb and spread the stuffing over the inside surface of the boned meat; roll the lamb up as tightly as you can and hold the meat in place with the aid of skewers and string. Rub the meat with garlic and insert thin slices under the skin using the point of a knife. **At this point the lamb can be kept in a cool place and roasted the next day.** Place the shoulder on a rack in a roasting pan. Put in a pre-heated 'hot' oven (425F Mark 7) and immediately reduce the heat to 'moderate' (350F Mark 4). Allow about 35 minutes to the pound plus an additional 20 minutes. Baste from time to time. If your guests are late and the lamb ready too soon, wrap meat up in tinfoil and keep hot in a cool oven. Serve with brown sauce or simple gravy, see pages 124, 125.

**Method.** Half-whip the cream, stir in the sugar and add the drops of vanilla. In another bowl beat the egg whites until they are stiff. Fold the egg whites carefully into the cream mixture and pour into an ice-cream tray or soufflé dish. Place in the freezing compartment of the refrigerator. To ensure perfect smoothness, beat the ice-cream with a fork just before it hardens. Serve decorated with chopped burnt almonds and pass the chocolate sauce round in a jug.

## Baked Avocado Pears with Crab Meat

*The stuffing can be prepared 1 day ahead   Action time 20 minutes*
*Cooking time 20–25 minutes*

2 avocado pears
3 tablespoons dry breadcrumbs
1 oz butter
4 tablespoons lemon juice
*Crab stuffing*
4 ozs crab meat

$\frac{1}{2}$ pint (1$\frac{1}{4}$ cups U.S.) béchamel sauce, page 123
1 teaspoon curry powder
salt
freshly ground pepper

## Coq au Vin

*Can be made 1 day ahead   Action time 40 minutes   Cooking time 45 minutes*

3$\frac{1}{2}$ lb chicken jointed
4 rashers streaky bacon diced
6 ozs mushrooms
$\frac{1}{2}$ pint (1$\frac{1}{4}$ cups U.S.) red wine (burgundy)
$\frac{1}{4}$ pint ($\frac{5}{8}$ cup U.S.) chicken stock
4 tablespoons brandy (optional)
1 onion finely chopped
1 clove garlic, minced or pounded

2–3 tablespoons beurre manié, page 133
flour
3 tablespoons olive oil
1 oz butter
1 bay leaf
$\frac{1}{8}$ tablespoon thyme
4 cloves
salt and freshly ground pepper

## Orange Cream Soufflé Surprise

*Can be made 1 day ahead   Action and cooking time 30 minutes*

2 eggs
$\frac{3}{8}$ pint ($\frac{15}{16}$ cup U.S.) milk
juice and grated rind of 1 large orange and 1 lemon ($\frac{1}{8}$ pint $\frac{5}{16}$ cup U.S.)
2 teaspoons gelatine (enough to set $\frac{2}{3}$ pint about 1$\frac{1}{2}$ cups U.S.)
3 tablespoons castor sugar
$\frac{1}{4}$ pint ($\frac{5}{8}$ cup U.S.) double cream

**Method.** *Crab stuffing:* make the béchamel sauce and remove it from the fire. Add the crab meat, salt, pepper and curry powder. **The sauce can be kept and reheated the next day; thin, if necessary, with a little milk.** *Baked avocado pears with crab meat:* cut the avocados in half, slicing from top to bottom and remove the stones. Pour a tablespoon of lemon juice in each half and tip the pear from side to side to cover all the exposed flesh. Fill each avocado half with the crab mixture. Melt the butter in a saucepan, add the breadcrumbs and fry for 1 minute before sprinkling over the avocado. Bake in a 'warm' oven (325F Mark 3) for 20–25 minutes.

**Method.** Heat half the oil in a flameproof casserole and gently fry the diced bacon and chopped onion for about 5 minutes. Meanwhile dust the chicken joints with flour. Remove the onion and bacon from the casserole and keep them in a warm place. Put the remaining oil in the casserole and brown the chicken joints for a few minutes on each side. Add the onion and bacon to the chicken. If you are using brandy pour it over the chicken at this point and set it on fire. When the brandy has ceased flaming, add the red wine, stock, thyme, cloves, salt, pepper, bay leaf and garlic. Bring the liquid to boiling point and then simmer over a low flame for 30–40 minutes or until the chicken is tender. At the end of the cooking time remove the chicken from the casserole and keep in a warm place. Add the beurre manié to the stock, stirring as you do so and simmer for a few minutes on top of the stove, then either add more beurre manié or cook fast for about 10 minutes to thicken the liquid by reducing it, stir from time to time. Meanwhile sauté the whole mushrooms in the butter and 1 tablespoon of water for about 5 minutes. Once the stock has thickened return the chicken to the casserole, add the mushrooms and either serve immediately or reheat the following day. For vegetables, choose new potatoes and braised chicory, page 115.

**Method.** Soak the gelatine in the milk for 5 minutes before slowly heating it in a pan until the gelatine dissolves; take care not to boil. Separate the yolks from the whites of egg. Put the yolks, fruit juice, rind and sugar together in a double boiler, or a basin over simmering water, and stir until the mixture begins to thicken; this will take about 10 minutes. Remove from the fire and stir from time to time until the mixture cools to blood temperature; add the milk, stirring as you do so. Whisk the egg whites until stiff; fold them carefully into the mixture, using a metal spoon and cutting through to the bottom of the bowl each time. Place in the refrigerator until the soufflé begins to set and hold its shape. Whip the cream until it is stiff. Next cover the base of a glass bowl with the soufflé mixture and spoon on the thick cream in four mounds. Cover the cream with the rest of the soufflé mixture and keep the bowl in the refrigerator until just before serving.

## Artichokes with Garlic Breadcrumbs

*Can be prepared 1 day ahead   Action time 30 minutes   Cooking time about 25 minutes*

6 globe artichokes
6 tablespoons dry breadcrumbs
6 ozs butter
6 cloves garlic minced or pounded
3 tablespoons finely chopped parsley
freshly ground pepper
1 teaspoon salt

## Vitello Tonnato

(VEAL WITH TUNNY SAUCE)

*Can be made 1 day ahead   Action time 40 minutes including sauce
Cooking time 1–1¼ hours*

2½ lbs boned, rolled shoulder of veal
2 ozs butter
watercress for garnish
*Tunny sauce*
1 small tin tuna fish (about 3½ ozs)
¼ pint (⅝ cup U.S.) single cream
½ pint (1¼ cups U.S.) egg mayonnaise

## Brandy Snaps

*Can be made 1 day ahead   Action time 25 minutes   Cooking time about 20 minutes*

4 ozs butter
5 ozs golden syrup
4 ozs demerara sugar
4 ozs flour
2 teaspoons powdered ginger
¼–½ pint (⅝–1¼ cups U.S.) double cream (filling)

For variation add chopped crystallized ginger or walnuts to the cream filling or use the Ginger Cream on page 32.

**Method.** Melt half the butter, add the garlic, breadcrumbs, salt and pepper and cook for 2–3 minutes. Remove the pan from the fire and stir in the chopped parsley. Trim about 1½–2 in. off the top of the artichoke leaves and open out the remaining part. Stuff the breadcrumb mixture down between the opened leaves with a small spoon and close them up by squeezing them together with your hands. **At this point the artichokes can either be stored until the next day or cooked immediately.** Place the artichokes in a steamer over boiling water and steam for 25–30 minutes. To keep hot, wrap in tinfoil and place in a warming drawer or very cool oven. Just before serving, melt the rest of the butter, put it in a small jug and pass it round with the artichokes. It is advisable to provide finger bowls for your guests – float a slice of lemon in each bowl.

**Method.** *Veal:* pre-heat the oven to 'hot' (425F Mark 7). Cover the veal with the butter and place it on a rack in a baking tray lined with tin foil. Put the meat in the oven and after 10 minutes reduce the heat to 'moderate' (350F Mark 4) and cook the meat for a total of about 1 hour–1 hour 15 minutes (allow 25–30 minutes to the pound depending on the thickness of the roll). Baste the veal from time to time during the roasting. Remove the meat from the oven and allow to cool. *Tunny sauce:* make 1 cup of thick mayonnaise using a mixture of lemon juice and tarragon vinegar, see page 127. Pound the tuna fish and add the cream or mix the tuna and cream together in a liquidizer. Blend the tuna fish mixture into the mayonnaise. **At this point wrap the veal in tinfoil, cover the bowl containing the sauce, and keep in a refrigerator or cool place until the next day.** An hour or two before sitting down to dinner, cut the veal in thin slices, place it on a serving dish and cover with the tunny sauce. Garnish the dish with sprigs of watercress. New potatoes and a chicory and lettuce salad go well with vitello tonnato. This is a perfect dish for a hot summer evening.

**Method.** Melt the butter in a saucepan. Remove the pan from the fire and add the rest of the ingredients, mixing them well together. Pour spoonfuls on to a greased baking tray, leaving plenty of space between each one. Bake in a 'warm to moderate' oven (325–350F Mark 3 4) until rich golden brown, which will take about 15–20 minutes. Remove from the oven and allow to cool for 1 minute before lifting with a spatula and placing on a board; quickly curl each brandy snap round a wooden spoon handle or a medium sized hair roller wrapped well in tinfoil. The latter, unconventional method produces excellent results. When the brandy snaps are still warm, but have hardened sufficiently to hold their shape, remove the spoon handles or rollers. Store in an airtight tin. An hour or two before serving, fill with whipped cream.

## Crab Mousse

*Make 1 day ahead   Action time and cooking time 15 minutes*

½ lb fresh crab meat
½ pint (1¼ cups U.S.) béchamel sauce, page 123
½ pint (1¼ cups U.S.) aspic jelly (Symington's)
¼ pint (⅝ cup U.S.) double cream
1 tablespoon lemon juice
salt
white pepper

## Baked Gammon with Apricots and Prunes

*The sauce can be made and the gammon partly cooked 1 day ahead   Action time 1 hour*
*Cooking time about 3½ hours*

4½ lbs gammon
10 large prunes
1 can apricots (about 15 ozs)
½ lb. demerara sugar
6 tablespoons golden syrup
about 30 cloves
dry mustard

*Sweet and sour sauce*
1 tablespoon arrowroot
juice from the can of apricots made up
  to 1 pint (2½ cups U.S.) with stock
  from the ham
2 tablespoons vinegar or lemon juice
2 tablespoons demerara sugar

## Lemon Meringues

*Can be made 1 day ahead   Action time 15 minutes   Cooking time about 1½ hours*

4 egg whites
8 ozs castor sugar
grated rind of 2 lemons
½ pint (1¼ cups U.S.) double cream whipped for filling
pinch of salt

**Method.** Make ½ pint of aspic jelly and ½ pint béchamel sauce and cool them both to blood temperature. Blend the crab meat and the béchamel sauce together; add the salt, pepper and lemon juice. Whip the cream and fold it into the crab mixture, and then blend in the aspic jelly. Pour the mousse into the dish in which you want to serve it and put it in the refrigerator.

**Method.** *Gammon and prunes:* soak the gammon for 3 hours in cold water. Pour boiling water on the prunes and leave them to soak for 6–8 hours. Remove the gammon from the water in which it has been soaked and place it in a large saucepan. Fill the pan with fresh, cold water and bring it slowly to the boil; simmer the gammon for 1½ hours. Remove the pan from the fire, take out the gammon and keep the liquid. With a knife cut the skin off the gammon and stick cloves in all over the exposed fatty surface. Cover the surface with dry mustard, golden syrup and then with brown sugar. You will find that this mixture tends to slide off but try to spoon back as much as you can. Place the gammon on a large piece of tinfoil and surround it with prunes and apricots, draw the edges of the foil together to cover the meat completely. **At this point the gammon can either be cooked immediately or kept until the next day.** Place in a 'warm' oven (325F Mark 3) for 1 hour (1½ hours if re-heating) and then cook the ham for 20 minutes in a 'hot' oven (425F Mark 7) having first removed the tinfoil. *Sweet and sour sauce:* blend the arrowroot with the vinegar or lemon juice in a bowl. Heat the apricot and ham stock together with the brown sugar and slowly pour this mixture on to the arrowroot stirring all the time. Return the mixture to the pan in which the liquid was heated and bring to the boil; simmer for 10 minutes. This sauce can easily be re-heated.

**Method.** Put the egg whites in a bowl, add a pinch of salt, and whisk them until they are very stiff. Shake in half the sugar and whisk again until stiff. Fold in the lemon rind and the rest of the sugar. Have ready a baking sheet covered with bakewell paper and spoon the meringue mixture on to the sheet with a dessertspoon to form small, shell shaped mounds. Cook in a 'very cool' oven (250F Mark ½) for the first 30 minutes and then reduce to (225F Mark ¼) and bake until the meringues feel firm and can be easily detached from the paper. Place the meringues on a wire rack until completely cool and then store in an airtight tin in a fairly warm place. Another method for making meringues is to whisk the whites until they are stiff and to add a teaspoon of sugar for each egg white and whisk again for about 10 seconds; the rest of the sugar and lemon rind is then folded in by hand. Sandwich the meringues together in pairs with the cream.

23

## Egg Mousse

*Make 1 day ahead    Action time 35 minutes including 'blender' mayonnaise*
*No cooking except for béchamel sauce*

$\frac{1}{2}$ pint (1$\frac{1}{4}$ cups U.S.) egg mayonnaise, page 127
$\frac{1}{2}$ pint (1$\frac{1}{4}$ cups U.S.) aspic jelly (Symington's)
$\frac{1}{2}$ pint (1$\frac{1}{4}$ cups U.S.) béchamel sauce, page 123
6 hard-boiled eggs
1 tablespoon lemon juice
1 tablespoon Worcestershire sauce
1 tablespoon chopped chives
salt and pepper

## Paupiettes de Porc

*Can be made 1 day ahead    Action time 60 minutes    Cooking time 40 minutes*

6 large pork fillet escalopes about
    6 in. square
1 pint (2$\frac{1}{2}$ cups U.S.) sauce espagnole,
    page 138
1 oz butter
*Stuffing*
3 ozs fresh breadcrumbs
$\frac{1}{2}$ lb minced pork

1 egg lightly beaten
1 teaspoon basil
$\frac{1}{2}$ small onion finely chopped
1 oz butter
parsley finely chopped

## Melon Baskets

*Fruit juice can be prepared 1 day ahead    Action time 40 minutes*

3 small ripe melons
2 peaches
$\frac{1}{2}$ lb strawberries
1 orange
1 lemon
2 tablespoons kirsch (optional)
2 tablespoons castor sugar
fresh vine leaves for decoration (optional)

**Method.** Make the béchamel sauce and aspic jelly and allow both to cool to blood temperature. Prepare the egg mayonnaise. Quarter the hard-boiled eggs and put the pieces in the bottom of a soufflé dish. Combine the mayonnaise with the béchamel sauce, and slowly blend in the aspic; add the lemon juice, Worcestershire sauce, salt and pepper and stir thoroughly. Pour the mixture over the eggs, sprinkle the surface with chopped chives, and leave to set. Serve accompanied with toast and butter.

**Method.** *Stuffing:* melt the butter and gently fry the onion for 5 minutes; add the minced pork and cook this for a further 5 minutes. Remove the pan from the fire and stir in the breadcrumbs, basil, parsley and lightly beaten egg. *Paupiettes de porc:* spoon a little stuffing on to the centre of each piece of pork and wrap the pork over to form a parcel, tucking in the sides; tie with thick cotton thread. The stuffing should first be cooled if the paupiettes are being prepared in advance. At this point they can be kept in a refrigerator or cool place until the next day. Melt some butter in a pan and fry the paupiettes for 3 minutes on each side. Meanwhile, heat the espagnole sauce, which can be thinned, if necessary, with a little stock. Put the paupiettes in a covered casserole with the sauce and place in a 'moderate' oven (350F Mark 4) for 30 minutes. Remove the cotton thread before serving. For speed use as an alternative to sauce espagnole: $\frac{1}{2}$ small onion finely chopped and fried in a little butter to which should be added 2 tablespoons flour; cook for 2 minutes, stirring all the time, and remove from the fire and slowly blend in 1 can tomatoes (about 14 ozs), $\frac{1}{4}$ pint ($\frac{5}{8}$ cup U.S.) red wine or cider, and $\frac{1}{4}$ pint ($\frac{5}{8}$ cup U.S.) stock. Add salt, pepper and a bay leaf. Return to the fire and cook until the sauce thickens.

**Method.** Start by squeezing the juice from the orange and lemon and add enough water to make up $\frac{1}{2}$ pint ($1\frac{1}{4}$ cups U.S.). Place the juice in a saucepan with the sugar and heat over a slow flame until the sugar has dissolved: remove from the heat and leave to cool. Meanwhile cut the melons in two, half an inch off centre, then cut a complete, half-inch wide ring from the rim of the larger piece. From the melon halves and the melon ring remove the seeds and cut away the flesh to within $\frac{1}{8}$ in. of the skin. Divide the melon flesh into small, mouth-sized pieces, peel and slice the peaches and add the fruit to the cooled juice together with the kirsch. Secure the handles to the scooped, cut melon halves with cocktail sticks and slide fruit or vine leaves on to the sticks to hide the joins. Fill the baskets with the fruit and juice and decorate with the strawberries. Chill before eating and, if possible, serve on a bed of fresh vine leaves. Other combinations of fruit such as cherries and grapes can be used. This is an extravagant dish except when melons are at their cheapest.

## Cold Mackerel with Mayonnaise

*Can be made 1 day ahead   Action time 40 minutes including mayonnaise
Cooking time about 30 minutes*

3 mackerel
juice of $\frac{1}{2}$ a lemon
2 tablespoons olive oil
freshly ground pepper
salt
$\frac{1}{4}$–$\frac{1}{2}$ pint ($\frac{5}{8}$–1$\frac{1}{4}$ cups U.S.) egg mayonnaise, page 127


## Pigeon Casserole

*Can be made 1 day ahead   Action time 30 minutes   Cooking time 1$\frac{1}{4}$ hours*

6 pigeons
$\frac{3}{4}$ pint (1$\frac{7}{8}$ cups U.S.) stock or cube
$\frac{1}{4}$ pint ($\frac{5}{8}$ cup U.S.) red wine
2 sticks celery cut in $\frac{1}{2}$ in. lengths
$\frac{1}{4}$ lb green bacon cut in $\frac{1}{2}$ in squares
1 large onion finely chopped

1 oz butter
flour
2 bay leaves
bouquet garni
salt, freshly ground pepper
beurre manié, page 133


## Oeufs à la Neige

*Can be made 1 day ahead   Action time 35 minutes   Cooking time about 40 minutes*

6 eggs
2 pints (5 cups U.S.) milk
2 tablespoons sugar
the grated rind of 1 lemon

26

**Method.** Ask your fishmonger to clean the mackerel. Wash the inside of the fish under running water and dry off any excess moisture. Place the mackerel on a large sheet of tin foil, sprinkle with the oil and lemon juice, add the salt and pepper and bake in a 'moderate' oven (350F Mark 4) for 25–30 minutes. Take the mackerel out of the oven and remove their skins while they are still warm. Next fillet them carefully and remove all bones. Serve cold sitting on a bed of lettuce leaves accompanied by mayonnaise.

Cold mackerel make a good supper dish; allow one each and ask your fishmonger to leave the head on.

**Method.** Melt the butter in a large flameproof casserole and fry the onion until transparent, add the celery and bacon and continue cooking for a few minutes. Meanwhile cut the pigeons in half through their backbones and flour each piece liberally. Place the pigeon halves in the casserole and brown them on each side. Add the stock, wine, salt, pepper, bay leaves and bouquet garni and heat to simmering point, reduce the heat and continue cooking over a low flame or in a 'cool' oven (280F Mark 1–2) for about $1\frac{1}{4}$ hours. At the end of the cooking time remove the pigeons from the casserole and keep in a warm place. Reduce the stock by boiling it for 10 minutes; stir from time to time. Taste, adjust seasoning and return the pigeons to the casserole. This is the most satisfactory thickening method. Alternatively, the stock can be thickened by the addition of a little beurre manié. This dish can be reheated the next day.

**Method.** Slowly bring 1 pint of milk to scalding temperature in a saucepan or frying pan. Meanwhile separate the whites from the yolks of egg and whisk the whites until they are stiff; fold in 1 tablespoon of sugar. With a spoon drop small mounds of egg white on the hot milk. Poach for about 1 minute on each side, and drain in a colander; keep the remaining milk in the pan on one side. Next gently beat the egg yolks in a bowl and add 1 tablespoonful of sugar. Add fresh milk to that used for poaching to make $1\frac{1}{2}$ pints. Pour the milk on to the egg mixture and lightly beat. Place the bowl over a pan of simmering water, add the lemon rind and cook the custard, stirring from time to time until it thickens enough to coat the back of a wooden spoon; this will take about 40 minutes. Remove from the fire and cool. This custard is much the same consistency as thick pouring cream and should be served well chilled, with the poached egg whites floating on top.

27

## Fish Pâté

*Make 1 day ahead   Action time 20 minutes   No cooking*

2 small buckling
¼ pint (⅝ cup U.S.) single cream
6 ozs butter
3 ozs smoked cod's roe
1 teaspoon brandy
1 tablespoon lemon juice
white pepper
lettuce, paprika and black olives (optional garnish)

## Duck Casserole with Oranges and Cider

*Make 1 day ahead   Action time 35 minutes   Cooking time about 1 hour 25 minutes*

1 duck (4½–5 lbs when dressed)
1 whole orange and the juice and
  grated rind of 2 oranges
1 pint (2½ cups U.S.) cider
4 tablespoons sugar
5 tablespoons flour

2 bay leaves
¼ teaspoon thyme
¼ teaspoon sage
salt
freshly ground pepper

## Chocolate Pots

*Can be made 1 day ahead   Action and cooking time 15 minutes*

¼ lb plain chocolate
3 eggs
1 tablespoon rum or 1 tablespoon orange juice
  and the grated rind of a medium-sized orange

**Method.** Remove the skin and bones from the buckling and the skin from the cod's roe. Cut the butter into small pieces. Place all the ingredients in a liquidizer and blend thoroughly. If no liquidizer is available, beat the butter to a cream and work in the buckling and smoked cod's roe, then add the cream, brandy, lemon juice and pepper. Put the mixture in a very small soufflé dish and leave to set in the refrigerator. To turn out, place the dish or tin in a pan of boiling water for about 30 seconds. Sprinkle with paprika and cut in four slices. Serve each slice on a bed of lettuce and add one or two black olives, for decoration. This pâté is the consistency of butter icing and should be served with toast.

**Method.** Place the duck's giblets in a baking tin and partially cover them with water. Put the duck on a trivet and cook it over the giblets in a 'hot', preheated oven (425F Mark 7) for 25 minutes. Remove from the oven and when the duck has cooled a little divide it into four and place the pieces in a medium-sized flameproof casserole. Keep the giblet stock. Meanwhile blend the flour in a basin with the orange juice and rind. Heat the cider in a saucepan and when it reaches simmering point pour it on to the orange juice and flour stirring all the time. Return the mixture to the saucepan, add the thyme, sage, bay leaves, salt and pepper and cook until the sauce thickens. In another saucepan boil the sugar with 4 tablespoons of water until it becomes dark brown and caramelizes; quickly add the orange and cider sauce. Once the caramel and sauce have blended together, remove the pan from the fire. Add ½ pint (1¼ cups. U.S.) giblet stock to the sauce and pour it over the duck. Simmer the duck over a low flame for about 1 hour until the flesh is tender. If the stock needs further thickening remove the duck pieces from the casserole and keep in a warm place. Boil the stock for about 10 minutes to reduce it, and stir from time to time. Remove the pan from the fire and replace the duck pieces, allow to cool. **At this point keep the duck casserole in a refrigerator or other cool place until the next day.** Before reheating, skim off the layer of fat which will have formed. Finally peel the third orange and warm the quarters through with the duck in the casserole.

**Method.** Melt the chocolate in a bowl over water which has just boiled. Separate the whites from the yolks, and blend the yolks and rum, or orange juice and rind, into the chocolate. Cool to blood temperature. Whisk the egg whites until stiff and fold them into the chocolate mixture; spoon into individual ramekin dishes or small glass bowls and chill. Serve with sponge finger biscuits.

## Cod with Crab Sauce Mornay

*Can be prepared 1 day ahead    Action and cooking time 25 minutes*

$\frac{3}{4}$ lb cod fillet
$\frac{1}{4}$ lb fresh crab meat
$\frac{3}{4}$ pint (1$\frac{7}{8}$ cups U.S.) milk
4 heaped tablespoons grated cheddar cheese
3$\frac{1}{2}$ tablespoons flour
2 ozs butter
1 tablespoon sherry
4 tablespoons dry breadcrumbs
salt and freshly ground pepper

## Pork Chops with Anchovies

*The anchovy butter can be made 1 day ahead    Action time 30 minutes*
*Cooking time 35 minutes*

6 pork chops
3 ozs butter
2 eggs lightly beaten
dried breadcrumbs
seasoned flour

*Anchovy butter*
8 anchovy fillets
3 ozs butter
freshly ground pepper
spring of parsley, finely chopped

## Blackcurrant Ice-cream

*Make 1 day ahead    Action time 15 minutes    Cooking time 15 minutes*

$\frac{1}{2}$ lb blackcurrants
4 whites of egg
$\frac{1}{2}$ pint (1$\frac{1}{4}$ cups U.S.) double cream
10 tablespoons castor sugar

**Method.** Put the milk in a pan with the salt and pepper and poach the cod slowly for about 10 minutes. Take the pan from the fire, drain and reserve the milk and skin and bone the fish. In another saucepan melt $\frac{3}{4}$ oz butter, remove from the fire, add the flour and mix to a smooth roux; cook for 1–2 minutes over a low flame stirring as you do so. Take the pan off the stove and slowly blend in a little of the milk in which the fish has been cooked. Return the pan to the fire, add the rest of the milk and stir until the sauce thickens. Add the cheese and cook for a few minutes. Put the crab meat and sherry in the sauce and remove the pan from the heat. Season with salt and pepper. **At this point the fish mixture can be kept until the next day, reheated over a low flame and thinned if necessary with a little milk.** Put the cod into scallop shells or ramekins with a 3 in. diameter and spoon the sauce over. Sprinkle with breadcrumbs, put a knob of butter on each and grill for 5 minutes.

**Method.** *Pork chops:* dip the chops first in flour, then in egg and lastly in the breadcrumbs which should be well pressed in. Melt the fat in a pan; fry the chops for a few minutes on each side until the coating is rich brown. Place them, with any remaining fat from the pan, in an ovenproof dish with a lid. **At this point the chops can either be put on one side for an hour or cooked immediately.** Place the chops in a 'moderate' oven (350F Mark 4) for 35 minutes. *Anchovy butter:* pound the anchovies and blend them well with the butter, pepper and chopped parsley. *Pork chops with anchovies:* a knob of anchovy butter should be placed on each chop just before serving. Mashed potatoes and braised chicory go particularly well with this dish.

**Method.** Place the blackcurrants with 4 tablespoons of sugar in a double boiler or basin over simmering water. Cook until the currants burst; this should take about 15 minutes. Strain the fruit and the juice through a sieve and allow to cool. Half-whip the cream and in a separate basin beat the egg whites until stiff. Mix the sieved blackcurrants and 6 tablespoons of sugar with the cream; fold in the egg white using a metal spoon and cutting through to the bottom of the basin. Put the mixture into a soufflé dish or on ice tray and place in the ice-making compartment of the refrigerator. For perfect smoothness, beat with a fork just before the ice-cream hardens.

## Barbecue Ribs with Sweet Spiced Sauce

*Sauce can be made 1 day ahead    Action time 30 minutes    Cooking time 1 hour 5 minutes*

3 lbs barbecue (spare) ribs
2 tablespoons soy sauce
*Sauce*
6 ozs demerara sugar
2 tablespoons soy sauce

¼ teaspoon chilli powder
¾ teaspoon ground cloves
¾ teaspoon French mustard
2 tablespoons cornflour
freshly ground pepper


## Stuffed Peppers

*Can be made 1 day ahead    Action time 45 minutes    Cooking time 1¼ hours*

6 large peppers
¾ lb minced beef
¾ lb sausage meat
¾ cup (1⅕ cup U.S.) cooked rice
1 medium onion finely chopped
¼ lb mushrooms thinly sliced
2 ozs peanuts
1 large tin tomatoes (about 2¼ lbs)

¼ pint (⅝ cup U.S.) red wine (optional)
1 teaspoon paprika
1 rounded tablespoon cornflour
2 ozs dripping or butter
1 teaspoon sugar
2 bay leaves
freshly ground pepper
salt


## Profiteroles au Chocolat

*The chocolate sauce and cream can be made 1 day ahead    Action time (including cream and sauce) 1¼ hours    Cooking time 20 minutes*

8 tablespoons plain flour
3 ozs butter
⅜ pint (1⅘ cup U.S.) water
3 eggs lightly beaten

pinch of salt
Chocolate sauce II, page 130
Chocolate cream, page 130


As a quick, easy alternative try Ginger Cream Log: 7 ozs ginger snap biscuits, ¾ pint (1⅞ cups U.S.) double cream, 4 tablespoons sherry, 1 white of egg, crystallized ginger for decoration.
*Method:* Whip ½ pint of cream until stiff. Dip the biscuits in the sherry, then butter with whipped cream and sandwich together to form a log; completely coat with cream, cover and leave in the refrigerator until the next day. An hour or two before serving whip the remaining cream and white of egg in separate bowls; blend together and give the log a further coating. Decorate with crystallized ginger.

Stuffed
Tomatoes

Steak &
Kidney Pudding

**Method.** *Barbecue ribs:* plunge the ribs into boiling water and cook for 3 or 4 minutes. Remove the pan from the fire, drain the ribs and brush with soy sauce. Place them on a rack in a baking tray and bake uncovered in a 'moderate' oven (350F Mark 4) for 1 hour. *Sauce:* blend the cornflour with 2 tablespoons of water in a saucepan and add the rest of the ingredients. Place the saucepan on the heat and bring to the boil; simmer for 10 minutes. To reheat, place the sauce in a bowl over simmering water. *Barbecue ribs with sweet spiced sauce:* place the ribs on individual plates and cover with sauce. Your guests will need finger bowls. Fill the bowls with warm water and float a slice of lemon in each bowl.

**Method.** Place the fat in a frying pan and fry the onion slowly for a few minutes. Add the mushrooms and peanuts and continue cooking for 5 minutes. Next put the sausage meat, minced beef, salt and pepper in the pan and cook for a further ten minutes; remove from the fire and add cooked rice. While the meat is cooking, carefully cut the stalks out of the peppers and remove the seeds. Stuff the peppers with the meat mixture and place them in a large casserole. Open the tin of tomatoes and put these together with the paprika, bay leaves, sugar and red wine in the casserole with the peppers. Add salt to taste. Simmer on top of the stove or in a 'very cool' oven (250F Mark $\frac{1}{2}$) for about $1\frac{1}{4}$ hours. To thicken the sauce before serving, mix 1 heaped tablespoon of cornflour with $\frac{1}{8}$ pint water ($\frac{5}{16}$ cup U.S.) and add this mixture to the tomato sauce stirring gently as you do so; simmer for 2 to 3 minutes. If reheating this dish, cook initially for 1 hour and reheat on top of the stove for 30 minutes. Serve with plain boiled rice.

**Method.** Sieve the flour. Put the fat, salt and water together in a saucepan and bring to the boil. Remove from the fire and add the flour; beat immediately with a wooden spoon until the paste is smooth and leaves the sides of the pan. Cool to blood temperature. Add the beaten eggs to the paste a little at a time beating thoroughly as you do so. If the eggs are large do not use the last spoonful as it may make the mixture too wet. When the paste is ready it should be smooth and shiny looking and able to hold its shape firmly. Put in small teaspoonfuls on a buttered baking tray. Bake for 20 minutes in a 'fairly hot' oven (375–400F Mark 5–6). When quite firm take out of the oven and place on a wire rack to cool. Make a small slit in the side of each one and, using a forcing bag or a small teaspoon, fill with chocolate cream. Put the profiteroles in a bowl and cover with chocolate sauce. These can be made several hours beforehand.

## Kipper Pâté

*Can be made 1 day ahead    Action and cooking time 15 minutes*

2 packets frozen kipper fillets (about 6 ozs each)
½ lb butter cut in small pieces
2 tablespoons lemon juice
2 tablespoons cream or top of the milk
pepper

Half the above ingredients are ample for 4.

## Stuffed Courgettes, Aubergines and Tomatoes

*Can be prepared 1 day ahead    Action time 1 hour    Cooking time 1½ hours*

*Vegetable cases*

| | |
|---|---|
| 6 large, firm tomatoes | 4 tablespoons cooked rice |
| 3 aubergines | 1 onion finely chopped |
| 6 courgettes | pulp from the vegetable cases |
| 4 tablespoons dried breadcrumbs | 1 teaspoon thyme |
| cooking oil | 1 teaspoon tarragon |
| *Stuffing* | 2 tablespoons chopped parsley |
| ½ lb. minced veal | 1 clove minced or pounded garlic |
| ½ lb. minced pork | salt and freshly ground pepper |
| 2 ozs mushrooms thinly sliced | 1 tablespoon cooking oil |

## Raisins avec Crème Chantilly

*Can be prepared 1 day ahead    Action time 50 minutes    No cooking*

1½ lbs grapes
1 tablespoon brandy
½ pint (1¼ cups U.S.) double cream
¼ teaspoon vanilla
2 tablespoons icing sugar
strips of angelica for decoration

**Method.** Cook the kippers according to the instructions on the packet and transfer the entire contents, with the exception of half the kipper skin, which should be discarded, into the blender. Add the butter, cream, lemon juice and pepper and blend thoroughly. Pour the kipper mixture into a small soufflé dish or individual ramekins and keep in a refrigerator or cool place. Garnish with parsley and serve with toast and butter.

If you use fresh kippers, poach a pair of large kippers for 10 minutes in a $\frac{1}{4}$ pint of liquid. Remove the bones and half the skin from the kippers and place the remaining kipper flesh and skin in a blender together with 2 tablespoons of the liquid in which the kippers were cooked. Add the other ingredients listed above and blend well.

**Method.** *Vegetable cases:* blanch the aubergines and courgettes for 5 minutes in boiling salted water. Cut the tops off the tomatoes and a thin slice lengthways off the courgettes; keep the tops and slices on one side. Cut the aubergines in half. Scoop out the interiors of the vegetables, chop the pulp into small pieces and keep for the stuffing. *Stuffing:* heat the oil in a pan and gently fry the onion until it is transparent, then cook the mushrooms. Add the minced meat, thyme, tarragon, garlic, vegetable pulp, salt and pepper and cook slowly for 10 minutes. Remove the pan from the fire and add the rice and parsley. *Stuffed aubergines, courgettes and tomatoes:* stuff the vegetable cases with the minced meat mixture. Place the lids on the courgettes and tomatoes and sprinkle breadcrumbs on the aubergines. **At this point the vegetable cases can either be cooked immediately or kept until the next day.** Put the vegetables in casseroles or in baking tins lined with tinfoil, first placing 1–2 tablespoons cooking oil on the bottom of each container. Cover with lids or tinfoil and bake the courgettes and aubergines in a 'moderate' oven (350F Mark 4) for $1\frac{1}{4}$ hours and the tomatoes for 30 minutes. 20 minutes before the end of the cooking time uncover the vegetables to allow them to brown a little. Serve with tomato sauce, see page 125, mashed potatoes and a green salad.

**Method.** First place the grapes in a bowl and cover them with boiling water; leave to stand for 1 minute to loosen the skins. Remove the skins, cut the grapes in half and take out the seeds. Whip the cream until it is stiff and add the vanilla, icing sugar and brandy. **At this point the ingredients can be kept in covered containers in the refrigerator until the next day.** Mix the grapes and cream together and place in a glass bowl. Decorate with thin strips of angelica and serve well chilled.

## Cold Consommé with Mock Caviar and Soured Cream

*Action time 15 minutes    No cooking*

1 tin (about 1¾ ozs) Danish 'caviar style' lumpfish roe
1 tin (about 10½ ozs) of beef consommé
¼ pint (⅝ cup U.S.) soured cream
1 lemon

## Fried Chicken

*Chicken can be jointed day before    Action time 30 minutes (does not include jointing)*
*Cooking time 20 minutes plus – depends on size of frying basket*

3½ lb chicken, preferably not frozen
1 egg lightly beaten
flour
dried breadcrumbs
salt and pepper
cooking oil for deep frying

## Hatch House Summer Pudding

*Make 1 day ahead    Action and cooking time 30 minutes*

¾ lb blackcurrants
3½ tablespoons sugar
¼ pint (⅝ cup U.S.) water
about 3 ozs crustless bread
½ pint (1¼ cups U.S.) custard sauce, page 129

**Method.** Place the tin of consommé in the refrigerator and chill it well. Cut the lemon in two, squeeze one half and slice the other to use as a garnish. Divide the ingredients equally between four small dishes or ramekins. Start by placing a layer of consommé in each dish, next add the lemon juice, then a layer of soured cream and lastly put a teaspoon of caviar in the centre of each portion. Make a small nick in each slice of lemon so that it can balance for decoration on the side of the dish. It is most important to keep this dish in the refrigerator until a few minutes before serving as the consommé will turn to liquid in a warm temperature.

**Method.** Joint the chicken into eight pieces. Trim off surplus bone and skin. Dip each piece first in the flour, which should be seasoned with salt and pepper, then in the egg and lastly in the breadcrumbs which should be pressed well in. Shake gently before cooking to remove the surplus crumbs. Heat the oil until a faint haze rises from the pan. Immerse the chicken pieces in the oil and cook for 20 minutes. Put the cooked chicken on absorbent paper to drain off excess oil. Serve with mashed potatoes and ratatouille, page 113 or watercress and lettuce salad.

Fried chicken is at its best when eaten straight from the pan, however, it will keep hot satisfactorily in a cool oven. Try to arrange to finish the frying only a few minutes before your guests arrive.

**Method.** Remove the stalks from the blackcurrants and put them in a saucepan with the sugar and water and bring slowly to the boil; simmer for 3–4 minutes and then remove from the heat. Line a one-pint pudding basin with bread. Fill the basin with half the fruit, cover with a layer of bread, add the rest of the fruit and juice, then another layer of bread. Cover with a piece of tinfoil and sit a heavy weight on top; if the juice tries to overflow, stand the basin on one side until the bread has absorbed the excess juice. Leave in a refrigerator or other cool place for 24 hours before turning out on a plate and covering with custard sauce.

## Buckling Pâté

*Make 1 day ahead    Action time 25 minutes    No cooking*

2 medium-sized buckling
$\frac{1}{4}$ pint ($\frac{5}{8}$ cup U.S.) double cream
$\frac{1}{4}$ lb butter
1 tablespoon horse-radish sauce
1 tablespoon lemon juice
paprika
freshly ground pepper
chopped chives or parsley for decoration

## Bœuf en Croûte*

(FILLET OF BEEF IN PUFF PASTRY)

*Action time 30 minutes    Cooking time 40 minutes*

2 lbs rolled fillet (preferably barded)
1 lb puff pastry**, page 133
$\frac{1}{2}$ lb mushrooms finely sliced
$\frac{1}{4}$ lb pâté
1 tablespoon brandy or sherry
4 ozs butter
freshly ground pepper
1 egg yolk lightly beaten for brushing pastry

*This is an expensive but easy dish; put the fillet into the oven 10 minutes before the guests are seated for dinner.
**Frozen pastry can be used.

## Caramel Oranges

*Oranges can be prepared 1 day ahead    Action time 30 minutes    Cooking time 5 minutes*

6 medium sized oranges
Caramel
6 ozs white sugar
$\frac{1}{4}$ pint ($\frac{5}{16}$ cup U.S.) water

**Method.** Remove the skin and the bones from the buckling. Whip the cream until it is stiff and cut the butter into small pieces. Place the buckling, butter, cream, lemon juice, horse-radish, paprika and pepper in a liquidizer and blend thoroughly. If a liquidizer is not available pound the buckling with the butter and then slowly blend in the cream and other ingredients. Pour into a small soufflé dish and put in the refrigerator to set. Decorate with chopped chives or parsley and eat with toast and butter. This pâté is very rich and creamy.

**Method.** Cook the mushrooms in 2 tablespoons of water and 1–2 ozs fat until they are soft; add the brandy or sherry and remove from the fire. Melt the remaining fat in a roasting pan, place the fillet in the pan and roast for 15 minutes in a 'moderate' oven (350F Mark 4), baste if fillet has not been barded. Lift from the pan and allow to cool slightly; remove fat, skewers and string. Roll out puff pastry to a thin sheet. Place the fillet on the pastry; spread the fillet with the pâté and mushrooms and liberally cover with freshly ground pepper before wrapping over the pastry. **At this stage the wrapped fillet can, if necessary, be kept for an hour or more before final cooking.** Brush the pastry with egg yolk and place in a 'hot' oven (425F Mark 7) and cook 20–25 minutes for medium rare beef. Serve with brown sauce, page 124, courgettes, new potatoes and green salad.

**Method.** Oranges: peel the oranges and remove all the pith. Cut the oranges into rings, extract the pips, and place the rings in a flat ovenproof dish. Scrape away all the pith from the zest of $\frac{1}{2}$ an orange and cut the zest into thin strips with a pair of scissors or a sharp knife. **The oranges and zest can be kept until the next day in an airtight container in the refrigerator.** *Caramel:* boil the sugar and water together in a saucepan and add the finely cut zest; watch carefully, especially as the syrup begins to turn colour, stir and remove from the fire immediately it becomes toffee colour. Pour the boiling syrup, which sets quickly, over the oranges.

If you would prefer to have syrup rather than a crunchy sheet of caramel covering the oranges, use double the quantity of sugar and cook initially without water, stirring from time to time; immediately the sugar turns toffee colour, remove the pan from the stove and very slowly and carefully add the water. Return the pan to the heat and simmer for 1 or 2 minutes before removing from the fire. Cool slightly before covering the oranges.

(The fastest way to clean the saucepan is to fill it with warm water and heat until the caramel melts.)

## Consommé Mousse

*Make 1 day ahead   Action time 25 minutes   No cooking*

3 tins (about 10½ ozs each) beef consommé
4 packets (about 3 ozs each) Philadelphia cream cheese
4 hard-boiled eggs cut in pieces (optional)
2 teaspoons curry powder
chopped chives

## Roast Turkey

*The stuffing can be prepared 1 day ahead   Action time, including preparation of stuffings, 1¼ hours   Cooking time 5½–6 hours*

12 lb turkey
chestnut stuffing, page 137
forcemeat stuffing, page 136
¼ lb butter

## Christmas Pudding

*Make several weeks ahead   Action time 45 minutes   Cooking time 8 hours*

4 ozs breadcrumbs
4 ozs flour
½ lb suet
½ lb currants
½ lb sultanas
½ lb raisins
3 ozs candied peel
4 ozs demerara sugar

2 ozs almonds blanched and chopped
rind of ½ lemon grated
pinch of salt
pinch of mixed spice
1 grated apple
3 large or 4 small eggs
⅜ pint (1⅝₆ cup U.S.) stout

**Method.** Put the Philadelphia cream cheese, hard-boiled eggs, curry powder and $\frac{2}{3}$ of the consommé together in a blender. Blend thoroughly and pour the mixture into ramekin dishes with a $2\frac{1}{2}$ in. diameter. Sprinkle with a few chopped chives and place in the refrigerator to set. Once the mousse has set firm pour on the remaining consommé. If the consommé has jellified, either remelt it by heating the tin in a pan of water, or spoon it on to the mousse, breaking the consommé up with a fork to cover the surface.

**Method.** Stuff the turkey at both ends and sew up the bird using a needle and strong thread. Cover the breast with butter and then loosely cover with foil. Place the turkey in a baking tin in a 'cool' oven (300F Mark 2) and baste it from time to time. A young frozen bird may cook in $3\frac{1}{2}$ hours, an older one from a farm can take up to 5 hours. When it is nearly ready, about 15 minutes before the end of the cooking time, remove the foil and cook in a fairly 'hot' oven (400F Mark 6) to brown the bird. Serve with bread sauce, page 126 and simple gravy, page 125.

**Method.** Mix all the ingredients together except the eggs and stout. Beat the eggs in a bowl and add the stout. Pour the egg mixture on to the other ingredients and and stir them well together. Put the mixture into a 2 pint pudding basin and cover with tinfoil. Steam for about 6 hours taking care the saucepan does not boil dry. Remove the pudding from the steamer and keep in a dry, cool atmosphere until required. On the day it is to be eaten return it to the steamer and cook for a further 2 hours. Serve with brandy butter, page 131.

# Lunch Party Menus
*(Serve 6 except where indicated)*

| | | |
|---|---|---|
| Hot Grapefruit with Brown Sugar<br>Braised Shoulder of Lamb with Ratatouille<br>Gâteau avec Crème au Chocolat | *pages* | 44–45 |
| | | |
| Apple, Celery and Prawn Cocktail<br>Kidney Casserole with Sausages<br>Biscuit Flan | | 46–47 |
| | | |
| Grapefruit and Prawn Cocktail<br>Moussaka<br>Marsala Cream | *(Serves 4)* | 48–49 |
| | | |
| Avocado Cream with Prawns<br>Rabbit with Prunes and Apples<br>Batter Pudding | | 50–51 |
| | | |
| Oeufs en Cocotte<br>Steak and Kidney Pudding<br>Pear and Grape Compôte | | 52–53 |
| | | |
| Salad Niçoise<br>Boiled Bacon with Sweet Cider Sauce<br>Summer Pudding | | 54–55 |
| | | |
| Stuffed Tomatoes<br>Fish Pie<br>Ginger Pudding | *(Serves 4)* | 56–57 |

Squid Vinaigrette                                     *pages*   58–59
Quiche Lorraine
Coffee Meringue Flan

Steamed Fish Soufflé                    (*Serves* 4)          60–61
Goulash
French Apple Flan

Buckling with Cheese and Tomatoes                      62–63
Lamb Chops en Croûte
Lemon Syllabub

Quick Mushroom Soup                                    64–65
Chicken and Ham Mousse
Caramel Custard with Raisins

Taramasalata                            (*Serves* 4)          66–67
Mild Chicken Curry
Marmalade Curd

In the lunch menus which follow steak and kidney pudding, boiled bacon and kidney and sausage casserole can be found among the main courses, and ginger and batter steamed puddings are also included. Most of the other menus are suitable as alternatives for dinner but tend to be less expensive than those in the dinner part section; rabbit and minced meat feature in the ingredients, as well as stewing steak. Some of the first courses are particularly simple such as quick mushroom soup, taramasalata and buckling with cheese and tomatoes.

## Hot Grapefruit with Brown Sugar

*Action time 30 minutes    Cooking time 10 minutes*

3 large grapefruit
6 tablespoons demerara sugar
6 tablespoons sherry
1 oz butter

## Braised Shoulder of Lamb with Ratatouille

*Ratatouille can be made 1 day ahead    Action time 40 minutes    Cooking time 2–2¼ hours*

4 lbs shoulder of lamb boned and
   rolled
1 clove garlic thinly sliced
*Ratatouille*
2 onions
1 aubergine
1 green pepper
5 courgettes
1 can tomatoes (about 14 oz)

parsley finely chopped
2 cloves minced garlic
2 bay leaves
1 teaspoon basil
1 teaspoon paprika
2 tablespoons olive oil
salt and freshly ground pepper
beurre manié, page 133

## Gâteau avec Crème au Chocolat

*Can be made 1 day ahead    Action and cooking time 35 minutes*

6 ozs plain chocolate
2 tablespoons sugar
4 eggs
1 oz butter
6 tablespoons cornflour

21 sponge finger biscuits – about 6 ozs
¼ pint (⅝ cup U.S.) milk
1 tablespoon rum (optional)
½ pint (1¼ cups U.S.) double cream
burnt hazelnuts or almonds, page 141

**Method.** Cut each grapefruit in half. Loosen the pulp from the peel with a grapefruit knife and cut the segments into mouth-sized pieces. An hour or two before serving pour 1 tablespoonful of sherry over each half and cover with brown sugar. Dot with butter and grill under a medium heat for about 10 minutes.

**Method.** *Lamb:* pre-heat the oven 'fairly hot' (400F Mark 6). Make incisions in the skin of the lamb and insert the garlic. Place the lamb in a baking pan and roast in the oven for 35 minutes. *Ratatouille:* either the day before or while the meat is cooking, finely chop the onions and slice the pepper, first removing the seeds. Also slice the aubergines and courgettes. Heat the oil in a fireproof casserole and fry the onion slowly for 5 minutes. Add the sliced pepper, courgettes and aubergines together with the minced garlic, bay leaves, paprika, salt, pepper and basil; put the lid on the pan and cook for a further 10 minutes. At the end of that time remove the casserole from the heat and add the tomatoes. *Braised shoulder of lamb with ratatouille:* sit the lamb in the middle of the ratatouille and cook in a 'warm' oven (325F Mark 3) for $1\frac{1}{2}$–$1\frac{3}{4}$ hours. Just before serving, remove the meat from the vegetables and if necessary add a little beurre manié to thicken the ratatouille; cook for 2 to 3 minutes and sprinkle with parsley. Cut the lamb in thick slices and serve on a large dish surrounded by ratatouille.

**Method.** Melt the chocolate and butter with $\frac{1}{3}$ pint ($\frac{7}{8}$ cup U.S.) of water in a saucepan and remove it from the heat. Meanwhile mix the cornflour and sugar together with 4 tablespoonfuls of milk. Separate the egg yolks from the whites and beat the yolks lightly. Add the beaten yolk to the cornflour and pour this mixture on to the melted chocolate, stirring hard. Return to the fire and cook for a few minutes until the mixture becomes difficult to stir and comes away from the sides of the pan. Remove from the heat and cool to blood temperature. Beat the egg whites until stiff and fold into the chocolate cream. Dip the sponge fingers into the remaining milk, to which the rum can be added. Cover the bottom of a cake tin (diameter 6 in. with movable base) with sponge fingers; spoon on a layer of chocolate cream, cover with another layer of biscuits and top with the rest of the cream. Chill in the refrigerator. This cake does not set solid, but with care can easily be moved to a plate with the aid of a palate knife. Cover with whipped cream and decorate with hazelnuts.

## Apple, Celery and Prawn Cocktail

*The mayonnaise can be made 1 day ahead*   *Action time 15 minutes – time includes*
*making 'blender' mayonnaise*   *No cooking*

6 ozs prawns
2–3 sticks celery
enough to make 1 cup (1¼ cups U.S.)
2 hard eating apples
enough to make 1 cup (1¼ cups U.S.)
½ pint (1¼ cups U.S.) egg mayonnaise, page 127
few drops tabasco
½–1 teaspoon tomato paste
lettuce leaves for garnish

## Kidney Casserole with Sausages

*Can be made 1 day ahead*   *Action time 30 minutes*   *Cooking time about 30 minutes*

12 lamb's kidneys
1 lb pork chipolata sausages
½ lb mushrooms finely sliced
1 pint (2½ cups U.S.) stock or cube
¼ pint (⅝ cup U.S.) red wine (or
additional stock)
2 tablespoons minced onion

5 tablespoons flour
2 ozs butter
2 bay leaves
salt and freshly ground pepper
few drops gravy browning

## Biscuit Flan

*Can be made 1 day ahead*   *Action time 20 minutes*   *Cooking time 10–15 minutes*

6 ozs digestive biscuits
½ lb raspberries or other soft fruit*
¼ lb butter
3 tablespoons sugar
1 teaspoon flour
¼ pint (⅝ cup U.S.) whipped cream

*As an alternative spread the surface of the flan with black currant jam and cover with cream.

**Method.** Cut the apple and celery into ¼–½ in. cubes. Add the tabasco and tomato paste to the mayonnaise and mix well. Put the apple, celery and prawns in the bowl with the mayonnaise and stir together. Cut the lettuce leaves into strips about ½ in. wide. Line the bottom of 6 glasses with the lettuce and cover with the prawn mixture. Serve with brown bread and butter. If the prawns are frozen, make sure they have completely defrosted before using, otherwise their moisture will dilute the mayonnaise.

**Method.** Remove the white membrane from the kidneys; wash them thoroughly and cut into thin slices. Melt 1 oz of butter and gently fry them for 1 minute on each side. Place the kidneys and their juice in a warmed ovenproof dish. Next divide each chipolata into two by squeezing the centre and giving two or three twists before cutting with a pair of scissors. Place the sausages in the frying pan and cook until the skins have browned, this will take about 5–10 minutes. Add the sausages to the kidneys and discard the fat in the pan. Return the pan to the stove, heat the remaining butter and sauté the mushrooms and onion together for a few minutes. Stir in the flour and cook this for 2 minutes before carefully blending in the stock and adding the bay leaves, salt, pepper and gravy browning. Bring the stock to boiling point, add the wine and pour it over the kidneys. Place in a pre-heated 'moderate' oven (350F Mark 4) and cook for 20 minutes. This dish can be reheated in the oven or brought to simmering point over a low flame. Serve with plain boiled or spiced rice and braised chicory, pages 120, 115.

**Method.** Crush the biscuits into fine crumbs with a rolling pin and put them in a mixing bowl. Meanwhile melt the butter in a saucepan. Add the melted butter, flour and sugar to the crumbs in the bowl. Have ready a well greased flan tin with a movable bottom. Cover the bottom and sides of the tin evenly with crumbs pressing firmly as you do so. Bake for 10–12 minutes in a 'fairly hot' oven (375F Mark 5). Remove the flan from the tin, cool and store in a cake tin. An hour or two before serving, spread the cream over the surface of the flan and spoon the raspberries or other fruit on top.

# Lunch Party for 4

## Grapefruit and Prawn Cocktail

*The mayonnaise can be made and the grapefruit prepared 1 day ahead*
*Action time 20 minutes   No cooking*

2 grapefruits
4 ozs prawns
$\frac{1}{4}$ pint ($\frac{5}{8}$ cup U.S.) egg mayonnaise page 127
few drops tabasco
$\frac{1}{4}$ teaspoon tomato paste
salt and freshly ground pepper
1 cup (1$\frac{1}{4}$ cups U.S.) shredded lettuce

## Moussaka

*Can be prepared 1 day ahead   Action time 40 minutes   Cooking time 45 minutes*

1 lb minced lamb or beef
$\frac{1}{4}$ lb sliced mushrooms
3 medium-sized aubergines
1 onion finely chopped
4 tablespoons grated parmesan cheese
1 oz butter
1 tablespoon Worcestershire sauce
2 tablespoons tomato paste
pepper and salt

1 teaspoon basil
4 tablespoons cooking oil
flour
*Sauce*
1 pint (2$\frac{1}{2}$ cups U.S.) milk
2 eggs lightly beaten
4$\frac{1}{2}$ tablespoons flour
1$\frac{1}{2}$ ozs butter
pepper and salt

## Marsala Cream

*Can be made 1 day ahead   Action and cooking time 15 minutes*

3 egg yolks
4 tablespoons castor sugar
3 tablespoons marsala or sweet sherry
$\frac{1}{4}$ pint ($\frac{5}{8}$ cup U.S.) double cream

48

Salad Niçoise

Salmon Mould

**Method.** Halve the grapefruits and hollow them out. Use only half the grapefruit flesh cut in small pieces, first removing as much as possible of the skin and pith. Dry the grapefruit pieces with a cloth to remove any excess juice. **At this stage the grapefruit can be kept in a covered container until the next day.** Mix the mayonnaise, tabasco, tomato paste, salt and pepper and add the grapefruit and prawns. Put a little shredded lettuce in the bottom of each hollowed out grapefruit and spoon the prawn mixture over. Serve with brown bread and butter. If the prawns are frozen, make sure they have completely defrosted before using, otherwise the moisture will dilute the mayonnaise.

**Method.** Put the aubergines in boiling water for 5 minutes, drain and cut into slices $\frac{1}{4}-\frac{1}{2}$ in. thick; dust with flour. Heat the butter and half the oil in a pan and gently fry the aubergines for 10 minutes. Remove them from the pan and keep on one side. Place the rest of the oil in the pan and fry the onions until they are transparent; add the mushrooms and cook for a few minutes. Next add the meat, tomato paste, Worcestershire sauce, basil, pepper and salt and cook gently for 20 minutes stirring from time to time. Line a $4\frac{1}{2}$ pint casserole with some aubergine slices, add the meat and cover with the remaining aubergines. Sprinkle with parmesan cheese. **At this stage the preparation can either be completed or the dish put on one side until the next day.** Make 1 pint of béchamel sauce, page 123 and remove the pan from the fire. Add the lightly beaten eggs to the sauce and blend them carefully. Pour the sauce over the contents of the casserole, cover with a lid, and cook in a 'moderate' oven (350F Mark 4) for 45 minutes.

**Method.** Put the yolks in a medium-sized mixing bowl, add the sugar and marsala or sherry and whisk over a saucepan of simmering water. Make sure that the water does not touch the bottom of the bowl. Continue whisking until the egg mixture is light and thick enough to hold the marks of the whisk for 8 or 9 seconds; this will take about 5 or 6 minutes. Remove the bowl from the heat and continue to whisk for another 5 minutes until the mixture cools to blood temperature. Half-whip the cream and fold it into the now cooled egg mixture. Pour into individual glasses and chill. Serve with small macaroons, page 135.

## Avocado Cream with Prawns

*Action time 15 minutes    No cooking*

2 ripe avocados
4 ozs prawns
¼ pint (⅝ cup U.S.) double cream
2 tablespoons vinaigrette sauce, page 128
lemon juice
salt
freshly ground pepper
paprika for decoration

## Rabbit with Prunes and Apples

*Can be made 1 day ahead    Action time 30 minutes    Cooking time about 2 hours*

3 lbs rabbit cut in pieces
12 prunes
1 large cooking apple, peeled and
  sliced
1 pint (2½ cups U.S.) cider
½ pint (1¼ cups U.S.) stock or cube
1 onion finely chopped
2 tablespoons vinegar

2 tablespoons olive oil
2 bay leaves
12 cloves
flour
1 oz butter
2 tablespoons cooking oil
beurre manié, page 133

## Batter Pudding

*Action time 15 minutes    Cooking time 1½ hours*

6 ozs flour
3 eggs
⅜ pint (1⁵⁄₁₆ cup U.S.) milk
3 ozs butter

**Method.** Cut the avocado pears in half and remove the stones. Scrape out all the flesh and crush it well with a fork. Whip the cream until it is thick and blend it with the avocado pear; add the vinaigrette sauce, lemon juice to taste, and the salt and papper. Mix in the prawns leaving a few on one side for decoration. Spoon into individual ramekin dishes, decorate with prawns and sprinkle with paprika. Serve with brown bread and butter.

**Method.** Soak the prunes for a few hours before cooking. Put the rabbit, cider, vinegar, oil, cloves and bay leaves in a bowl and leave to stand for 3 or 4 hours. Remove the rabbit from the marinade and dry off any excess moisture with a cloth; keep the marinade. Flour each piece of rabbit thoroughly. Meanwhile melt the butter in a medium-sized flameproof casserole and add the oil. Next fry the onion gently for about 5 minutes until it is soft. Add the rabbit pieces and brown them for 3 to 4 minutes on each side. Pour in the stock, add the marinade and prunes and heat to simmering point. Put a lid on the casserole and cook in a 'very cool' oven (250F Mark $\frac{1}{2}$) for 2 hours or until the rabbit is tender. 45 minutes before the cooking time is up, add the apple. If necessary, thicken the stock by adding a little beurre manié and blend it in, stirring carefully. This dish can be reheated. Serve with plain, boiled potatoes and baked carrots.

**Method.** Separate the yolks from the whites of egg. Put the flour in a basin and make a well in the middle. Melt the butter slowly in a saucepan. Place the egg yolks in the well, add the milk and mix to a thick batter. Pour the melted butter on to the batter mixture and stir thoroughly. Lastly whip the whites of egg until they are stiff and fold them into the batter. Butter a 2 pint pudding basin and pour the batter into this; cover with greaseproof paper or with tinfoil and steam over boiling water for $1\frac{1}{2}$ hours. Remember to check from time to time to ensure that the saucepan does not boil dry. Serve with pats of butter and brown sugar.

51

## Oeufs en Cocotte

*Action time 10 minutes   Cooking time 10 minutes*

6 eggs
¼ pint (⅝ cup U.S.) double cream
pinch of tarragon (optional)
salt
pepper freshly ground

## Steak and Kidney Pudding

*Can be prepared 1 day ahead   Action time 45 minutes*
*Cooking: 1st stage 1½–2 hours; 2nd stage 1½ hours*

1½ lbs best stewing steak
¾ lb ox kidney
½ lb mushrooms
2 ozs butter
seasoned flour
1 bay leaf

freshly ground pepper
*Suet crust*
12 ozs self-raising flour
6 ozs suet
2 teaspoons salt

## Pear and Grape Compôte

*Can be made 1 day ahead   Action and cooking time 30 minutes*

6 firm dessert pears
½ lb grapes
5 ozs sugar
juice of 1 lemon
1 teaspoon arrowroot
3 tablespoons strong china tea*
2 tablespoons pine nuts (optional)

*China tea adds an interesting smoky flavour and combines well with many kinds of fruit.

**Method.** Break the eggs into 6 buttered ramekin dishes. Put the cream and tarragon into a small saucepan and well season the cream with salt and pepper. Pre-heat the oven to 'fairly hot' (375F Mark 5). About 10 minutes before your guests sit down to dinner put the ramekins in a pan containing water which has recently boiled and place in the oven; they will take 8–10 minutes to cook. Just before you take the eggs out of the oven, heat the cream to scalding temperature. Pour a little cream over each egg and serve immediately.

**Method.** *Steak and kidney:* fry the mushrooms gently in the butter and 1 tablespoon of water for 5 minutes. Trim the meat and cut it into $1\frac{1}{2}$ in. squares. Cut the kidney into rather smaller pieces, having first removed the membrane. Roll the kidney and steak in seasoned flour and place in a flameproof casserole together with the mushrooms, bay leaf and freshly ground pepper. Cover with water and bring to simmering point, then either lower the heat and continue to cook on top of the stove or place in a 'very cool' oven (250F Mark $\frac{1}{2}$) for $1\frac{1}{2}$–2 hours. *Suet crust:* rub the flour, suet and salt lightly through your fingers before adding just enough water to hold the mixture together and enable it to be rolled out on a floured board. Line a 3 pint pudding basin, remembering to leave enough suet on one side to form a lid. **The preparation should halt at this point if the pudding is to be eaten the next day.** *Steak and kidney pudding:* put the stewed meat with the mushrooms, bay leaf and liquid into the lined basin and cover with the remaining suet. Place a piece of foil over the top of the basin and hold it down with a saucepan lid. Finally put the bowl in a steamer over boiling water and cook for $1\frac{1}{2}$ hours remembering to check from time to time to ensure the saucepan does not boil dry. Half-an-hour before the cooking time is up, gently raise a corner of the suet lid and add as much hot liquid as the pudding will hold; use hot stock or the water from the pan over which the pudding is cooking. It is not necessary to be exact about timing, extra steaming will not harm the pudding.

**Method.** Put the sugar in a saucepan with $\frac{1}{2}$ pint of water and bring it slowly to the boil; add the lemon juice. Peel and core the pears and cut them into quarters. Simmer these in the liquid for about 10–15 minutes or until the pears are tender and remove them from the pan. Blend the arrowroot with the tea and add to the liquid in the saucepan; simmer for two or three minutes. Take the pan off the stove, replace the pears and leave to cool. Meanwhile pour boiling water over the grapes and leave to stand for about 30 seconds to loosen the skins. Peel the skins off the grapes, cut them in half and remove the seeds. If you are preparing this compôte in advance keep the grapes in an airtight container in the refrigerator and add the grapes to the pears just before serving. The pine nuts should also be added at the last minute.

## Salad Niçoise

*Vegetables can be prepared 1 day ahead    Action time 20 minutes*
*No cooking apart from preparation of vegetables*

1 tin tuna fish (about 8 ozs)
1 tin anchovy fillets
½ lb cold boiled potatoes
½ lb cooked french beans
½ lb tomatoes
1 tablespoon capers
¼ lb black olives
3–4 tablespoons sauce vinaigrette, page 128
1 sprig mint finely chopped (optional)

## Boiled Bacon with Sweet Cider Sauce

*The sauce can be made 1 day ahead    Action time 20 minutes*
*Cooking time about 1 hour 35 minutes*

3 lbs bacon (collar)
*Sweet cider sauce*
¾ pint (1⅞ cups U.S.) cider
6 ozs red currant jelly
6 tablespoons demerara sugar
2¼ tablespoons flour
1½ teaspoons soy sauce
½ teaspoon ground cloves
1½ ozs butter

## Summer Pudding

*Make 1 day ahead    Action time 20 minutes    Cooking time about 10 minutes*

1 lb raspberries
½ lb red currants
3 tablespoons sugar
¼ pint (⅝ cup U.S.) water
6 ozs crustless white bread (about 7 or 8 slices)
½ pint (1¼ cups U.S.) custard sauce, page 129)

**Method.** Slice the boiled potatoes, cut the french beans in half, skin and quarter the tomatoes. Break the tuna fish up with a fork. Put the potatoes, french beans, chopped mint and tuna fish into a bowl and pour over the sauce vinaigrette; stir gently to mix the ingredients together. Add the tomatoes and mix again. Garnish with capers, black olives and anchovies – the latter can be arranged in a lattice pattern.

**Method.** *Boiled bacon:* place the bacon in a saucepan and cover with water. Bring the water to the boil, pour it away and start again with fresh boiling water. Simmer slowly for $1\frac{1}{4}$ hours. Take the bacon out of the pan and with a knife remove the skin. Cut the bacon in slices, place it in a shallow, ovenproof dish, cover with the sauce and put a lid on the dish; keep warm in a 'very cool' oven (225F Mark $\frac{1}{4}$). *Sweet cider sauce:* heat the cider, sugar and red currant jelly, and add the soy sauce and ground cloves. In another pan melt the butter, draw the pan aside from the stove and add the flour to form a roux. Return the pan to the heat and cook for 1 or 2 minutes before removing the pan from the fire and slowly blending in the cider mixture. Put the pan back on the heat and bring the sauce to the boil; allow to simmer for a few minutes before either pouring over the sliced bacon or keeping to reheat the next day.

**Method.** Remove the stalks from the red currants and put them in a saucepan with 3 tablespoons of sugar and $\frac{1}{4}$ pint of water and bring slowly to the boil; simmer for 3 minutes stirring from time to time and then add the raspberries and continue cooking and stirring for another 2 minutes before removing from the heat. Strain off the juice. Dip the bread in the juice and line a pudding basin. Place half the fruit in the bottom of the lined basin and cover with a layer of bread; add the rest of the fruit and top with a further layer of bread and any remaining fruit juice. Place a piece of tinfoil over the basin and sit a heavy weight on top. If the juice tries to overflow, wait until some of it has been absorbed by the bread. Leave to stand in the refrigerator or other cool place for 24 hours before turning out on to a plate and covering with custard sauce. This pudding is often served either with cream or custard but it is much more delicious eaten with both.

### Stuffed Tomatoes

*Can be prepared 1 day ahead    Action time 30 minutes    No cooking*

4 large or 8 medium-sized tomatoes  
1 can tuna fish (about 3¼ ozs)  
1 stick celery cut in ¼ in. squares  
6 tablespoons mayonnaise  
1 teaspoon minced onion  

salt  
freshly ground pepper  
pinch of tarragon  
few drops of tabasco  
watercress or parsley for decoration  

### Fish Pie

*Fish can be prepared 1 day ahead    Action time 45 minutes    Cooking time 20 minutes*

1 lb fresh haddock  
4 scallops  
¾ pint (1⅞ cups U.S.) milk  
¼ pint (⅝ cups U.S.) cider  
5 tablespoons flour  
1 small, finely chopped onion  

1½ ozs butter  
1 bay leaf  
¼ teaspoon mace  
salt and pepper  
potato crust, page 118  

### Ginger Pudding

*Action time 20 minutes    Cooking time about 1½ hours*

4 ozs self-raising flour  
4 tablespoons demerara sugar  
2 ozs butter  
6 tablespoons golden syrup  
1 egg lightly beaten  
⅛ pint (5/16 cup U.S.) milk  
2 teaspoons ground ginger

Method. Cover the tomatoes with boiling water and leave to stand for about 30 seconds to loosen the skins. Peel the skin from the tomatoes and put them in the refrigerator for about 20 minutes to firm them before stuffing. Drain the oil from the tuna fish. Cut the tops off the tomatoes and hollow out the interior. Keep the tops on one side; put the flesh in a bowl with the tuna fish, mayonnaise, celery, onion, tarragon, tabasco, salt and pepper and mix well. **At this point the tuna fish mixture and tomatoes can be kept in containers in the refrigerator until the next day.** Fill the hollow tomatoes and pile on as much of the tuna fish mixture as possible. Put the tops back on the tomatoes and decorate with sprigs of watercress or parsley. Serve with melba toast, page 134 and butter.

Method. Place the haddock, skin side uppermost, under a hot grill for 2 to 3 minutes. Remove the haddock from the grill and scrape off the skin, cut it into mouth-sized pieces and keep it on one side. Next wash the scallops and separate the orange from the white part. Gently remove the outside tissue and divide the white part into four. Put the milk, bay leaf, salt, pepper and mace together in a pan. Bring to the boil and simmer for a few minutes before adding both the white and orange parts of the scallops. Cook for 1 minute before removing from the heat. Strain the scallops and remove the bay leaf, keep the liquid, and put the scallops on one side with the haddock. Melt the butter in the pan and add the onion which should be cooked very slowly until it is transparent. Draw the pan aside from the heat and stir in the flour; return the pan to the fire and cook for a few minutes before again removing the pan from the heat and slowly blending in the milk. Heat the sauce over a low flame until it thickens and add the cider. Taste and adjust seasoning. **At this point the fish and sauce can be kept until the next day. Reheat the sauce before adding the fish, and, if necessary, thin it with a little more cider.** Add the haddock and scallops to the sauce and pour the mixture into a pie dish. Top with potato crust and bake in a 'moderate' oven (350F Mark 4) for 20 minutes. Just before serving slip the dish under a hot grill to brown the surface lightly. Eat with a green salad.

Method. Butter a one-pint pudding basin and put the golden syrup into it. Cream the butter and sugar together; blend in the egg. Pour the flour in slowly, beating all the time and add the ginger. Stir in the milk and beat again. Spoon the mixture into the syrup basin and cover the top with greaseproof paper or tinfoil and secure with string. Place in a steamer over simmering water and cook for $1\frac{1}{2}$ hours. Make sure that the saucepan does not boil dry. Serve with additional golden syrup.

## Squid Vinaigrette

*Can be made 1 day ahead   Action time 30 minutes   Cooking time 10 minutes – it will probably be necessary to grill the squid in two batches*

2½ lbs squid
olive oil
juice of 1 lemon
pepper and salt
6–8 tablespoons vinaigrette dressing, page 128
lettuce for garnish.

## Quiche Lorraine

*Can be prepared 1 day ahead   Action time 25 minutes   Cooking time 35–40 minutes*

6 ozs gruyère cheese
6 ozs bacon
¼ pint (⅝ cup U.S.) single cream
½ pint (1¼ cups U.S.) milk
3 eggs
pinch of nutmeg
¼ teaspoon oregano

freshly ground pepper
*Shortcrust pastry,* page 133
9 ozs plain flour
2¼ ozs butter
2¼ ozs lard
pinch of salt

## Coffee Meringue Flan

*Can be made 1 day ahead   Action time 30 minutes   Cooking time about 1¼ hours*

3 whites of egg
7 ozs castor sugar
2 teaspoons coffee essence
1 teaspoon vinegar
1 tin chestnut purée
½ pint (1¼ cups U.S.) double cream

**Method.** First clean the squid by pulling off the head and taking the skin off the bag-like part of the fish. Turn the bag-like part inside out and remove any remaining intestines and the transparent spine bone; wash thoroughly under a running tap. Next cut the tentacles from the head. Place the squid with the tentacles on a piece of foil; cover with oil, lemon juice, salt and pepper and grill slowly for 10 minutes, turning the squid once during this time. Put the fish and the juice in a basin to cool. When cold remove the squid from the basin and cut the bag-like part into rings with a pair of scissors. Add the vinaigrette dressing to the juice in the basin. Just before eating, place the squid on a bed of lettuce and cover with the dressing. Serve on individual plates.

**Method.** Make the pastry, roll it out on a floured board and line a large, buttered flan case with a moveable bottom (about 9 in. diameter). Dice the cheese into $\frac{1}{4}$ in. cubes and also dice the bacon. **If you are preparing this dish in advance put the diced bacon and cheese in covered containers, wrap the flan case in tinfoil and keep in the refrigerator or other cool place until the next day.** Lightly beat the eggs together in a bowl and add the milk, cream, oregano, nutmeg and pepper. Cover the bottom of the flan case with the diced cheese and bacon and pour over the egg mixture. Bake in a 'moderate to fairly hot' oven (350–375F Mark 4–5) for 35 to 40 minutes. Cool a little before serving with a green salad.

**Method.** Mix the coffee essence and vinegar together in a cup. Whip the white of egg until stiff. Taking great care, very slowly mix in the sugar and liquid by adding a few drops of liquid, alternating with about a heaped teaspoonful of sugar, and whipping at once after each addition; repeat the process until all the sugar and liquid has been added. Put the mixture on to a well buttered pyrex meat plate, keeping it higher at the sides than at the centre. Bake in a 'very cool' oven (250F Mark $\frac{1}{2}$) for about 30 minutes, then reduce the oven to (225F Mark $\frac{1}{4}$) and bake until quite firm, which will take 1 hour or more. **Allow the meringue flan to cool, before placing it in a plastic bag and storing in an airtight tin; do not try to remove it from the plate.** Just before serving cover the surface with chestnut purée and spoon over whipped cream.

## Steamed Fish Soufflé

*Action time 25 minutes   Cooking time 50 minutes*

¼ lb fresh haddock
¼ lb smoked haddock
generous ½ pint (1¼ cups U.S.) milk
2 ozs butter
4 eggs
5 tablespoons flour
salt and freshly ground pepper

This soufflé makes an excellent light supper dish for two or three people. Serve it with a green salad.

## Goulash

*Can be made 1 day ahead   Action time 30 minutes   Cooking time 1½–2 hours*

1½ lbs best stewing steak
2 large onions finely chopped
¼ pint (⅝ cup U.S.) red wine
¼ pint (⅝ cup U.S.) tomato juice
¼ pint (⅝ cup U.S.) stock or cube
¼ pint (⅝ cup U.S.) soured cream

2 ozs dripping
flour
1 bay leaf
1 tablespoon paprika
salt and freshly ground pepper
beurre manié, page 133

## French Apple Flan

*Pastry can be prepared 1 day ahead   Action time 30 minutes   Cooking time 30 minutes*

1 lb cooking apples
⅛ pint (5/16 cup U.S.) double cream
2 tablespoons sugar
1 egg
*Shortcrust pastry*
6 ozs plain flour
1½ ozs lard
1½ ozs butter
pinch of salt

**Method.** Poach the fish for 10 to 12 minutes in the milk. Take the pan off the heat, remove the fish and keep the milk. When the fish has cooled a little, take away the skin and bones and break the fish up with á fork. Separate the yolks from the whites of egg and lightly beat the yolks. Melt the butter in a saucepan, add the flour and mix to a smooth paste and cook for 1 or 2 minutes. Remove the pan from the fire and slowly blend in a little of the milk in which the fish has been cooked, having first made it up to half a pint. Return to the fire and, stirring all the time, add the rest of the milk. Bring to the boil and cook for 2 to 3 minutes before taking the pan off the stove and adding the beaten egg yolks, fish, salt and pepper. Allow the mixture to cool to blood temperature. Beat the egg whites until they are stiff and fold them carefully into the mixture using a metal spoon and cutting through to the bottom of the pan each time. Pour the soufflé into a 3 pint, greased pudding basin, cover the top of the basin with tinfoil or greaseproof paper and secure with string. Steam the soufflé for 50 minutes. If necessary it can continue steaming for a further 15 minutes without being ruined.

**Method.** Cut the steak into 1½ in. cubes and roll it in flour. Melt the fat in a flame-proof casserole and brown the meat for 3 minutes on each side. Remove the meat from the pan and keep in a warm place. Put the onion, salt, pepper and paprika in the casserole and fry the onion slowly until it is transparent; this will take about 5–10 minutes. In another saucepan warm the tomato juice, red wine, and stock together with the bay leaf. Return the meat to the casserole, add the warmed stock and simmer over a low flame for 1½–2 hours until the meat is tender. Stir in a little beurre manié to thicken the sauce if necessary. **At this point the goulash can be kept and reheated the next day.** Just before serving add the soured cream; do not allow to boil. This dish should be accompanied by rice, page 120.

**Method.** Make pastry in the usual way, see page 133. Roll the pastry out on a floured board and line a buttered 8 in. flan tin, which should preferably have a removable bottom. Peel and quarter the apples, remove the corc and cut the apples into thin slices. Arrange the slices, slightly overlapping each other, in a circular pattern on the pastry. Beat the egg, sugar and cream together in a bowl and pour this mixture over the apples. Bake in a 'fairly hot' oven (400F Mark 6) for 30 minutes. This apple flan is at its best when eaten warm rather than hot, so cool it a little before serving.

## Buckling with Cheese and Tomatoes

*Can be prepared 1 day ahead   Action time 20 minutes   Cooking time 5 minutes*

1 large or 2 medium-sized buckling
6 ozs grated cheddar cheese
$\frac{1}{4}$ pint ($\frac{5}{8}$ cup U.S.) single cream
4–6 tomatoes peeled and chopped
6 teaspoons brandy or sherry

## Lamb Chops en Croûte

*The sauce can be made and the chops prepared 1 day ahead   Action time 45 minutes
Cooking time 25 minutes*

6 boned loin of lamb chops
  (keep bones for sauce)
1 pint ($2\frac{1}{2}$ cups U.S.) brown sauce,
  page 138
14 ozs puff pastry,* page 133
6 ozs mushrooms thinly sliced

*Frozen puff pastry can be used.

1 small onion finely chopped
1 oz butter
1 lightly beaten egg – for brushing
  pastry
a pinch of rosemary and thyme
salt and freshly ground pepper
parsley finely chopped

## Lemon Syllabub

*Can be made 1 day ahead   Action time 10 minutes   No cooking*

$\frac{1}{2}$ pint ($1\frac{1}{4}$ cups U.S.) double cream
3 tablespoons sherry or white wine
3 tablespoons castor sugar
juice $1\frac{1}{2}$ lemons
grated rind 1 lemon (for decoration)

62

**Method.** With a sharp knife remove the skin and bones from the buckling. Break the fish up and divide it equally between six ramekin dishes. Cover the fish with a layer of tomatoes, then add the cream, the brandy or sherry and top with the cheese. Grill until the cheese is golden brown, this will take about 5 minutes. Ideally this dish should be prepared in ramekins with a 3 in. diameter.

**Method.** Grill the boned chops for 3 minutes on each side to brown them. Remove them from the heat and set on one side to cool. Meanwhile melt the butter in a pan and gently fry the onion for 5 minutes. Add the mushrooms, 2 tablespoons of water, the parsley, rosemary, thyme, freshly ground pepper and a little salt and cook until the water has been partially absorbed by the mushrooms. Take the pan off the stove and let the mushroom mixture cool. Roll out the pastry until it is thin and cut it into six strips about 8 in. long. Place the chops on the pastry strips and spoon a share of the mushroom mixture on to each. Moisten one edge of the pastry with a little water and fold it over the chop, pressing it down firmly on the other side; then close in the sides. **At this stage the chops can be kept in a cool place until the next day.** Just before cooking, brush lightly with egg, place on a buttered baking tray and cook in a 'hot' oven (425F Mark 7) for 25 minutes. Start the cooking 10–15 minutes before you sit down to lunch. Serve with brown sauce, new potatoes and red cabbage, page 114.

**Method.** Place the lemon juice, the cream, sugar, sherry or white wine in a bowl. Whip with a rotary beater until thick and creamy. Place the syllabub in individual glasses and decorate with the grated lemon peel. Chill and serve with sponge finger biscuits.

If you want this recipe to go further, fold in a stiffly beaten white of egg.

## Quick Mushroom Soup

*Can be made 1 day ahead    Action and cooking time 20 minutes*

½ lb onions finely chopped
½ lb mushrooms
2 pints (5 cups U.S.) chicken stock or cube
3 ozs butter
2 tablespoons flour
freshly ground pepper
salt

## Chicken and Ham Mousse

*Make 1 day ahead    Action and cooking time 30 minutes, does not include chicken*

3 cups (3¾ cups U.S.) minced chicken
    (about 3½ lb boiled chicken, page 137)
1 cup (1¼ cups U.S.) minced boiled
    bacon or ham (about ¼ lb)
1 pint (2½ cups) chicken stock*
1½ teaspoons gelatine – enough to set
    ½ pint (1¼ cups U.S.)
¼ pint (⅝ cup U.S.) double cream

3 tablespoons egg mayonnaise,
    page 127, or Hellmann's
parsley finely chopped
celery salt
pepper
cucumber and sprigs of parsley for
    decoration

*If you are using a cube or poor quality chicken stock, double the quantity of gelatine.

## Caramel Custard with Raisins

*Make 1 day ahead    Action time 20 minutes    Cooking time 40 minutes*

1¾ pints (4⅜ cups U.S.) milk
4 tablespoons castor sugar
6 egg yolks
3 rounded tablespoons dessert raisins
5 sponge finger biscuits
2 drops vanilla essence
*Caramel*
4 ozs white sugar
4 tablespoons water

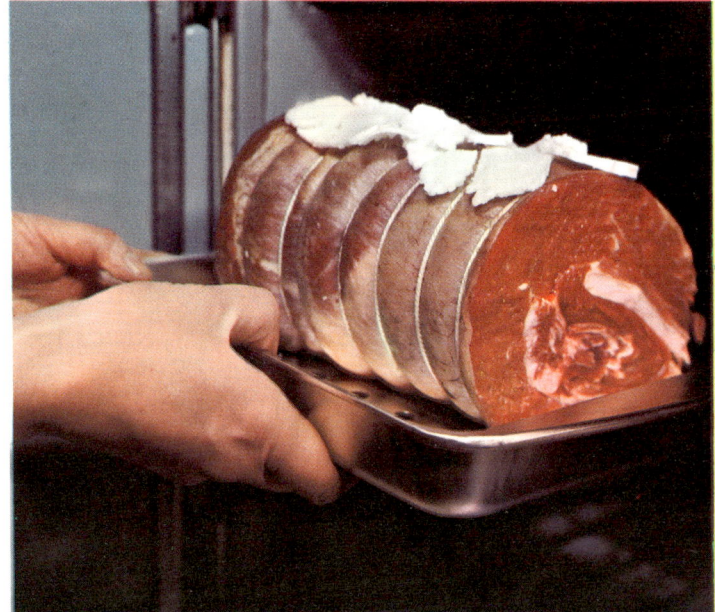

Oven-ready
Beef

Onion Soup

**Method.** Melt the butter in a saucepan and gently fry the onion until it is transparent; add the mushrooms and continue cooking for 5 minutes. Meanwhile heat the stock. Put the flour, mushrooms, onion and half the stock in a liquidizer and blend thoroughly. Transfer the soup back to the saucepan, add the rest of the stock and bring to the boil; season and continue cooking for another 3 to 4 minutes. This soup can also be made with the use of a Mouli, in which case the flour must be added to the mushrooms and onion at the end of the first stage of cooking; cook the flour for a few minutes, add the stock and put the mixture through the Mouli. Reheat and simmer for 3 or 4 minutes before serving.

**Method.** Soak the gelatine in the chicken stock and then heat the mixture over a low flame to dissolve the gelatine, taking care the stock does not boil. Remove from the fire and cool to blood temperature. Add the chicken, ham, parsley, celery salt and pepper. Half-whip the cream and blend it into the chicken mixture together with the mayonnaise. Keep in a refrigerator or other cool place. Decorate with parsley and slices of cucumber. Serve with new potatoes and a selection of salads, one of which should be green, page 111.

**Method.** Bring the milk, raisins, vanilla drops and sugar to the boil in a saucepan; cool slightly. While the milk is cooling, boil the sugar and water for the caramel in a cake tin until the syrup turns deep golden brown. Remove from the fire and place the sponge finger biscuits in the caramel. Next gently beat the egg yolks and, stirring all the time, pour on the milk. Transfer the custard to the tin containing the caramel and bake in a 'fairly hot' oven (375–400F Mark 5–6) for 40 minutes. Remove from the oven and chill. Turn out by first placing the tin in a bowl of nearly boiling water for about 30 seconds to partly melt the caramel.

65

### Taramasalata

*Can be made 1 day ahead   Action time 20 minutes   No cooking*

½ lb smoked cod's roe*
2 tablespoons single cream
2 tablespoons olive oil
juice of 1 lemon
1 teaspoon finely chopped chives

2 tablespoons fresh white breadcrumbs
pepper
black olives and lettuce
  (optional garnish)

*For smoked cod's roe in a jar, use the recipe on page 89.

### Mild Chicken Curry

*Can be made 1 day ahead   Action time 45 minutes   Cooking time about 2 hours*

3½ lb chicken
1½ pints (3¾ cups U.S.) chicken stock
  or cube
1 onion finely chopped
4 tablespoons cooking oil
1 tablespoon brown sugar
1 clove garlic minced or pounded
  (optional)
1 tablespoon tomato paste
3 ozs coconut cream† or 6 tablespoons
  desiccated coconut*

flour
salt
*spices***†
1 tablespoon paprika
1 tablespoon turmeric
⅛ teaspoon chilli powder
2 teaspoons ground cumin
2 teaspoons ground cardamom
2 teaspoons ground coriander
1 teaspoon ground ginger

*Bring the stock to the boil and pour it over the desiccated coconut; leave to stand for 1–2 hours and strain through a sieve pressing as much coconut through as possible.
†Available from Indian Emporium, 8 Great Russell St. London W.C.1. who also accept mail orders.
**As a substitute use curry powder.

### Marmalade Curd

*Can be made 1 day ahead   Action and cooking time 35 minutes*

4 ozs butter
3 ozs marmalade
8 tablespoons castor sugar
3 eggs well beaten
the grated rind and juice of a lemon
¼ pint (⅝ cup U.S.) double cream (decoration)

**Method.** Remove the skin from the smoked cod's roe. Pound it and blend in the other ingredients either by hand or in a liquidizer. Sprinkle with chopped chives. Taramasalata can either be put in a dish and passed round the table or it can be spooned on to a bed of lettuce, garnished with black olives and served on individual plates. It should be eaten with toast and butter.

**Method.** Cut the chicken in 8 pieces and flour liberally. Heat half the oil in a saucepan or a flameproof casserole and brown the chicken for a few minutes on each side. Take the chicken out of the pan and keep it warm. Put the rest of the oil in the pan and fry the onion and garlic slowly for 5 to 10 minutes together with all the spices and the coconut cream. Pour on the stock, add sugar, tomato paste and salt, and bring to the boil; reduce the heat, add the chicken and simmer slowly for 1½–2 hours (half an hour less if this dish is to be reheated). To thicken the sauce, either remove the chicken and keep it in a warm place while you cook the stock fast to reduce it, or thicken it with flour, see the instructions for beurre manié on page 133. Serve with poppadums, page 136 and mango chutney.

**Method.** Put the butter, marmalade, sugar, lemon juice and rind in a double boiler or in a bowl over simmering water and heat for 10 minutes stirring from time to time. Take off the fire and cool slightly before stirring in the beaten egg. Return to the heat and continue cooking over simmering water for about 25 minutes, until the mixture thickens sufficiently to coat the back of a spoon. Pour the mixture into glass bowls or ramekins and cool before decorating with whipped cream. Provide sponge fingers for your guests as this is a very rich, sweet dish.

# Fork Supper Menus

| | | | |
|---|---|---|---|
| Salmon Mould | *(Serves 10)* | *pages* | 70–71 |
| Meat Loaf | | | |
| Crème de Menthe Jelly | | | |

Onion Soup         *(Serves 10)*      72–73
Cold Roast Beef with Soured Cream, Olives and Lemon Slices
Lemon Soufflé

Vichyssoise         *(Serves 12)*      74–75
Stuffed Cabbage Rolls in Tomato Sauce
Chocolate Meringue Crumble

Chicken Liver Pâté         *(Serves 12)*      76–77
Blanquette de Veau
Fresh Fruit Salad

Thick Artichoke Soup         *(Serves 12)*      78–79
Curried Beef
Peaches with Cream and Caramel

Gazpacho         *(Serves 16)*      80–81
Cold Chicken in Mild Curry Sauce
Chocolate Cherry Gâteau

Smoked Cod Mousse         *(Serves 16)*      82–83
Terrine of Pork
Madame Pusich's Iced Pineapple Gâteau

Pâté Maison                          (*Serves 16*)          *pages* 84–85
Chicken and Almonds in Lemon Sauce
Lychees and Black Grape Salad


If a choice has to be made between giving a cocktail party or a fork supper party, there is little doubt that the latter is a far more satisfying way of entertaining. Fork supper parties are more work, but the budget-conscious may like to be reminded that they are often no more expensive to give than cocktail parties, especially if the drink is restricted to wine and a simple menu is chosen.

The quantities needed for the main dishes are dealt with in the menus, but here is a guide to the amount of salad and wine to provide. So far as salads are concerned, work on the principle of four to five mouth-sized pieces of lettuce or other green stuff per person, together with, say, half to three-quarters of a cup of winter or rice salad and a few slices of tomato or cucumber. As for the wine, although people's drinking habits vary considerably, you will find that between half and three-quarters of a bottle per person is generally enough to allow.

At a fork supper party it is a good idea to offer a choice of puddings and if you provide a fresh fruit salad in addition to something rich and creamy you will please most of your guests. A cheese board is also popular and a good basic selection would be Boursin Fines Herbes and Brie, together with two firmer cheeses such as Roquefort and English Cheddar. Serve with butter, several kinds of crisp biscuit and also sticks of celery.

## Fork Supper for 10

### Salmon Mould

*Make 1 day ahead   Action time 30 minutes   No cooking apart from white sauce*

2 tins salmon (about 7½ ozs each)
½ pint (1¼ cups U.S.) egg mayonnaise
  or Hellmann's
½ pint (1¼ cups U.S.) white sauce
½ pint (1¼ cups U.S.) water
1⅓ tablespoons gelatine (enough to set
  1⅓ pints, 3⅜ cups. U.S.)

2 tablespoons tomato paste
1 tablespoon Worcestershire sauce
2 teaspoons grated onion
2 teaspoons lemon juice
few drops tabasco
salt and freshly ground pepper

### Meat Loaf

*Make 1 day ahead   Action time 35 minutes   Cooking time 1¼ hours*

1½ lb minced beef
1 lb pork sausage meat
¼ pint (⅝ cups U.S.) milk
2 eggs
2 cups (2½ cups U.S.) fresh white
  breadcrumbs
1 large onion finely chopped
1 green pepper cut in ¼ in. cubes
3 or 4 large sprigs of parsley finely
  chopped

2 tablespoons cooking oil
1 teaspoon salt
2 teaspoons paprika
1 teaspoon basil
¼ teaspoon thyme
freshly ground pepper
*browned breadcrumbs for garnish*
10 tablespoons dried breadcrumbs
2 ozs butter

### Crème de Menthe Jelly

*Make 1 day ahead   Action and cooking time 30 minutes*

¾ lb sugar
juice and grated rind of 6 lemons
2 tablespoons gelatine (enough to set 2 pints, 5 cups U.S.)
1½ pints (3¾ cups U.S.) cider
few drops peppermint flavouring
few drops green colouring
½ pint (1¼ cups U.S.) double cream –
  decoration
a few walnuts – decoration

**Method.** Soak the gelatine in the water for 5 minutes and then slowly heat until it dissolves; take care to see the water does not boil. Allow the gelatine mixture to cool to blood temperature. Make the white sauce and also cool to blood temperature. Open the tins of salmon and strain off the juice. Put the salmon in a bowl and flake it with a fork. Slowly blend in the mayonnaise, white sauce and gelatine mixture and add the rest of the ingredients. Pour into two pint-sized moulds and leave to chill overnight. To serve, turn out on to plates and surround with a bed of water-cress or lettuce leaves.

**Method.** Heat the oil in a pan and cook the onion and green pepper together for 5–10 minutes. Put all the rest of the ingredients, with the exception of the milk, eggs and the browned breadcrumbs, together in a large bowl. Knead together with the hands until the ingredients are thoroughly mixed and add the onion and green pepper. Beat the eggs in the milk and then blend the milk into the meat mixture. Butter a 3 in. deep bread tin or casserole and pour in the meat loaf mixture; bake in a 'moderate' oven (350F Mark 4) for $1\frac{1}{4}$ hours. Pour off the surplus juice before turning out on a meat dish. Cover the top surfaces of the meat loaf with breadcrumbs, which have first been fried in butter until they are brown and slightly crunchy. To reheat, cover the meat loaf with tinfoil and place in a 'fairly hot' oven (375F Mark 5) for $\frac{3}{4}$ hour. This meat loaf can be eaten at once but it improves if kept and reheated the next day. Serve with brown sauce, page 124 or tomato sauce, page 125, mashed potatoes and a green salad.

**Method.** If the lemon juice makes less than $\frac{1}{2}$ a pint make up the difference with cider. Add the gelatine to the lemon juice and leave to stand. Meanwhile put the sugar in a saucepan together with $1\frac{1}{2}$ pints cider and bring slowly to the boil to melt the sugar. Remove from the heat and when just off the boil, pour on to the lemon juice, stirring as you do so. Add the rind together with the peppermint flavouring and green colouring. Pour the jelly into the bowl in which you wish to serve it and leave to set. Decorate with whipped cream and walnuts.

## Onion Soup

*Can be made 1 day ahead    Action time 35 minutes    Cooking time 1 hour 10 minutes*

2½ lbs onions thinly sliced
4¼ pints (10⅝ cups. U.S.) beef stock or cube
3 ozs butter
10 slices French bread
3 ozs grated gruyère cheese
2 tablespoons dry sherry or brandy (optional)
2 teaspoons sugar
salt and freshly ground pepper

## Cold Roast Beef with Soured Cream, Olives and Lemon Slices

*Can be prepared 1 day ahead    Action time 45 minutes    Cooking time about 1 hour*

4½ lbs rolled beef sirloin
¾ pint (1⅞ cups U.S.) soured cream
juice of 1 lemon
1 lemon cut in thin slices
½ lb black olives

## Lemon Soufflé

*Can be made 1 day ahead    Action and cooking time 45 minutes*

Juice and rind of 4 lemons
8 eggs
10 ozs castor sugar
4 teaspoons gelatine – enough to set 1⅓ pints (about 3¼ cups. U.S.)
1 pint (2½ cups U.S.) milk
½ pint (1¼ cups U.S.) double cream

**Method.** Melt the fat in the bottom of a fireproof casserole. Add the onion and gently stew it for 20 minutes. Pour on the stock, add the salt, pepper and sugar and bring to the boil. Place in a 'very cool' oven (275F Mark 1) for 50 minutes. Meanwhile toast the French bread on both sides under a low grill, sit the cheese on the top side and float in the onion soup for the last 20 minutes of the cooking time. Adjust the seasoning, add the sherry or brandy and serve. If preparing this dish in advance simmer it in the oven for only 30 minutes and reheat on top of the stove the next day while the bread is being prepared. As before, float the bread in the soup and bake in the oven for 20 minutes.

**Method.** Pre-heat the oven to 'very hot' (450–475F Mark 8–9). If meat is lean, cover with fat. Out on a rack in a baking pan and place in oven. Immediately reduce the heat to 'moderate' (350F Mark 4). Since cold roast beef should be very rare, the meat should not cook for more than 15 minutes to the pound. **At this stage the meat can be kept wrapped in tinfoil in the refrigerator as it should not be sliced and garnished more than a few hours before it is eaten.** Cut it in slices and then into strips about $\frac{3}{4}$ in. wide and $2\frac{1}{2}$ in. long, making sure you discard any gristle and other inedible parts. Place the meat on a large dish and cover with soured cream flavoured with the lemon juice. Decorate with black olives and lemon slices and serve with baked potatoes page 119 and a selection of salads see pages 111, 112. This dish is attractive to look at as the black olives and yellow lemons contrast well with the soured cream through which glimpses of pink beef can be seen.

**Method.** Crack the eggs and separate the yolks from the whites. Place the sugar, egg yolks, lemon juice and rind in a medium sized mixing bowl and cook over a saucepan of simmering water, stirring all the time. Continue stirring until the mixture thickens and coats the back of the spoon; this will take 20–25 minutes. Remove from the stove and beat from time to time until the mixture cools to blood temperature. Meanwhile soak the gelatine in the milk for a few minutes and then heat the milk slowly until the gelatine has dissolved; do not allow to boil. Cool milk to blood temperature and add to the lemon mixture stirring all the time. Beat the egg whites until stiff and half-whip the cream. Fold the cream and then the egg whites carefully into the milk and lemon mixture using a metal spoon and cutting through to the bottom of the bowl each time; pour into a soufflé dish and place in the refrigerator to set.

# Fork Supper for 12

## Vichyssoise

*Can be made 1 day ahead    Action time 20 minutes    Cooking time 40 minutes*

3 pints (7½ cups U.S.) chicken stock or
  cube
9 medium-sized leeks (white part only)
  cut finely
4–5 medium-sized potatoes thinly
  sliced
1½ onions finely chopped
2 sticks celery cut in pieces

¾ pint (1⅞ cups U.S.) single cream
2 ozs butter
parsley finely chopped
few drops tabasco
¾ teaspoon Worcestershire sauce
salt
chopped chives or watercress for
  decoration


## Stuffed Cabbage Rolls in Tomato Sauce

*Can be prepared 1 day ahead    Action time 40 minutes    Cooking time 1 hour*

2 large savoy cabbages (24–30 leaves)
*Stuffing*
3 lbs minced beef
1 cup (1¼ cups U.S.) fresh
  breadcrumbs
2 teaspoons thyme leaves
2 onions finely chopped
2 ozs dripping or butter
salt

freshly ground pepper
*Tomato sauce*
1 can tomatoes (1 lb 13 ozs)
½ pint (1¼ cups U.S.) cider
3 tablespoons flour
2 teaspoons Worcestershire sauce
1 teaspoon paprika
salt and pepper


## Chocolate Meringue Crumble

*Meringues can be made 1 day ahead    Action time 40 minutes*
*Cooking time about 1½ hours for each batch*

8 whites of egg
1 lb castor sugar
½ lb plain chocolate
1¼ pints (3⅛ cups U.S.) double cream
a few drops vanilla

As an alternative to chocolate use 2 tablespoons coffee essence to flavour the cream and leave out the vanilla.

**Method.** Melt the butter in a saucepan and gently fry the leaks and onion for about 5 minutes. Add the potatoes, celery, tabasco, Worcestershire sauce, parsley and salt and cover with chicken stock. Bring the stock to boiling point and simmer covered for 35 to 40 minutes, until the vegetables are tender and can either be rubbed through a sieve or blended in a liquidizer. Taste and adjust seasoning. Chill well and just before serving add the cream. Decorate with chopped chives or watercress.

**Method.** *Cabbage:* blanch the cabbage leaves for 4 minutes in boiling water and then drain and remove any hard stalk. Lay the leaves flat on a board to dry while the stuffing is being prepared. *Stuffing:* melt the fat in a saucepan and sauté the onions until they are soft; add the meat, thyme, breadcrumbs, salt and pepper and cook for a further 10 minutes. *Stuffed cabbage rolls:* put a good spoonful of stuffing on each cabbage leaf and roll it up to form a sausage shaped parcel. Place the stuffed leaves in a casserole. *Tomato sauce:* heat the tomatoes in a saucepan and add the the Worcestershire sauce, paprika, salt and pepper. Mix the flour with a little of the cider and when it is well blended add the rest. Pour the tomatoes on to the cider stirring as you do so; transfer the mixture to the saucepan, bring to simmering point and stir for 2 or 3 minutes. **At this stage the stuffed cabbage rolls and sauce can be kept in separate containers until the next day.** Just before cooking, pour the sauce over the cabbage rolls and cook in a 'warm to moderate' oven (325–350F Mark 3–4) for 1 hour. Serve with boiled rice to which a little turmeric has been added during the cooking. The turmeric turns the rice an attractive shade of pale orange and adds a pleasant aromatic flavour. Allow 2 ozs of rice per person.

**Method.** *Meringues:* make the meringues using the same method as for the lemon meringues on page 23. Since the meringues in this recipe are to be broken up there is no need to take any special care in spooning the mixture on to the baking tray. For 8 whites of egg it is easier to make the meringues in two batches. To store put the meringues in a plastic bag and keep in a tin in a warm, dry place. *Chocolate meringue crumble:* break the meringues in small pieces about the size of a walnut. Cut the chocolate finely with a knife; if a grater is used the attractive chocolate crunch will be lost. Whip the cream until it is stiff and add the drops of vanilla. About 1 hour before serving pour the cream over the broken meringue, add the chocolate and mix well together. Put the meringue crumble into individual glasses and serve with sponge finger biscuits.

### Chicken Liver Pâté

*Can be made 1 day ahead   Action and cooking time 15 minutes*

| | |
|---|---|
| $\frac{3}{4}$ lb chicken liver | 1 bay leaf |
| 6 ozs bacon | pinch of tarragon |
| 6 ozs butter | salt |
| 6 ozs mushrooms | freshly ground pepper |
| 2 cloves garlic | 2 tablespoons brandy (optional) |

### Blanquette de Veau

*Can be made 1 day ahead   Action time 45 minutes   Cooking time $1\frac{1}{2}$–2 hours*

| | |
|---|---|
| 4 lbs best pie veal | $1\frac{1}{2}$ ozs butter |
| $2\frac{1}{4}$ pints ($5\frac{5}{8}$ cups U.S.) chicken stock or cube | 1 bouquet garni |
| | $\frac{1}{4}$ teaspoon tarragon |
| 3 sticks celery sliced | salt and pepper |
| 3 carrots sliced | $\frac{1}{2}$ pint ($1\frac{1}{4}$ cups U.S.) single cream |
| 1 onion studded with cloves | 2 egg yolks |
| 3 slices lemon | 12 tablespoons beurre manié, page 133 |
| $\frac{3}{4}$ lb shallots | |
| $\frac{3}{4}$ lb button mushrooms thinly sliced | |

### Fresh Fruit Salad

*Sugar syrup and grapes can be prepared 1 day ahead   Action time 45 minutes Cooking time 15 minutes*

| Syrup | Fruit |
|---|---|
| 2 oranges | 2 oranges |
| 2 lemons | $\frac{1}{2}$ lb grapes |
| 10 tablespoons castor sugar | 3 cups ($3\frac{3}{4}$ cups U.S.) cubed melon or |
| 1 teaspoon arrowroot | pineapple |
| 2 tablespoons strong china tea* | 3 eating apples |
| | 3 bananas |
| | 2 tablespoons pine nuts (optional) |

A few fresh or frozen strawberries make a good addition as they add colour.
*See note on page 52.

**Method.** Trim off the bacon rind and cut each rasher into about four pieces. Peel the mushrooms and cut them in half. Squeeze or crush the garlic. Melt the butter in a saucepan and add the chicken livers, bacon, mushrooms, garlic, bay leaf, tarragon, salt and pepper and cook slowly for 15 minutes. Remove the bay leaf and pour the contents of the saucepan into a liquidizer, add the brandy and blend thoroughly. Spoon into a small pâté jar or soufflé dish and leave to set. Decorate with bay leaves and serve with toast and butter. Other recipes for liver pâté appear on pages 10 and 111.

**Method.** Trim the veal and cut it into $1\frac{1}{2}$ in. cubes. Place the veal in a pan of cold water, bring to the boil, and blanch for 2 minutes. Drain the veal and wash it under cold running water to remove the scum. Return the meat to the pan and add the celery, carrot, onion, slices of lemon, bouquet garni, tarragon, salt and pepper; cover with the stock. Bring the stock to simmering point and simmer for $1\frac{1}{2}$–2 hours until the veal is tender. Meanwhile boil the shallots for 10–15 minutes until tender but still firm, and fry the mushrooms gently in butter for 5 minutes. Remove and discard the vegetables, lemon slices and bouquet garni from the pan in which the veal is cooking. Add the beurre manié, a spoonful at a time, to thicken the stock and stir carefully. Next add the shallots and the mushrooms. **At this point the blanquette de veau can be kept and reheated the next day.** Just prior to serving, lightly beat the cream and the egg yolks together in a bowl and add to the stock; do not allow to boil. Serve with boiled rice and a green salad.

**Method.** *Syrup:* squeeze the juice from the lemons and oranges and make up to one pint with water. Put the juice in a saucepan with the sugar and bring slowly to the boil to melt the sugar; simmer for 10 minutes. Blend the arrowroot in a tablespoon of water; pour some of the hot juice on to the mixture stirring all the time. Add this mixture to the simmering juice in the saucepan and cook for 2 to 3 minutes. Remove the pan from the heat and allow the juice to cool. *Fruit:* peel the grapes, halve and de-seed them; peel and core the apples and cut them into $\frac{1}{4}$ in. cubes; cut the melon or pineapple into $\frac{3}{4}$ in. cubes, first removing the skin and the seeds; remove the zest, pith and seeds from the orange and cut into small pieces. *Fruit salad:* once the juice has cooled add the fruit, pine nuts and china tea. An hour or two before serving peel the bananas, cut them into thin slices and add to the fruit salad making sure that they are well covered with juice. Serve with pouring cream.
For those in a hurry a tin of grapefruit segments and a tin of lychees make a good alternative base for a fruit salad, in which case the melon or pineapple can be left out.

---

### Thick Artichoke Soup

*Can be made 1 day ahead   Action and cooking time 35 minutes*

4 lbs Jerusalem artichokes
$1\frac{1}{4}$ pints ($3\frac{1}{8}$ cups U.S.) milk
$2\frac{1}{2}$ pints ($6\frac{1}{4}$ cups U.S.) water
5 tablespoons flour
$1\frac{1}{2}$ ozs butter
salt and freshly ground pepper

### Curried Beef

*Can be made 1 day ahead   Action time 1 hour   Cooking time 2–$2\frac{1}{2}$ hours*

| | |
|---|---|
| $4\frac{1}{2}$ lbs stewing steak | flour |
| 4 onions finely chopped | salt |
| $3\frac{1}{2}$ pints ($8\frac{3}{4}$ cups U.S.) beef stock or | *spices*† |
| cube | $\frac{1}{2}$–$\frac{3}{4}$ teaspoon chilli powder |
| $\frac{1}{2}$ lb sultanas | 1 tablespoon turmeric |
| $\frac{1}{4}$ lb chopped walnuts | 2 tablespoons powdered ginger |
| 4 ozs dripping or butter | 1 tablespoon ground coriander |
| 7 ozs coconut cream† or 4 ozs | 2 teaspoons ground cardamom |
| desiccated coconut* | 2 teaspoons ground cumin seed |
| 2 cloves garlic minced or pounded | $\frac{1}{4}$ teaspoon ground cloves |
| 4 tablespoons demerara sugar | $\frac{1}{4}$ teaspoon cinnamon |
| 4 tablespoons tomato paste | |

†Available from the Indian Emporium, 8 Great Russell St., London W.C.1. who also accept mail orders. For hot curry add extra chilli powder.

*Bring the stock to the boil and pour it over the desiccated coconut; leave to stand for 1–2 hours and strain through a sieve pressing as much coconut through as possible.

### Peaches with Cream and Caramel

*Prepare 1 day ahead   Action time 30 minutes   Cooking time about 3 minutes*

12 peaches
1 pint ($2\frac{1}{2}$ cups U.S.) double cream
4 tablespoons brandy or sherry (optional)
$\frac{1}{2}$ lb demerara sugar

Grapes, with the skins and seeds removed, can also be used for this dish.

**Method.** Clean the artichokes and skin them as thinly as possible. Put them in a pan containing 2½ pints of boiling water, add a little salt and cook for 15 minutes or until the artichokes are soft. Meanwhile heat the milk to scalding temperature and melt the butter in another saucepan. Draw the pan containing the butter aside from the heat and blend in the flour to form a roux. Return the pan to the heat and cook for 1 to 2 minutes before removing the pan from the fire and blending in the milk; add salt and pepper. Return the pan to the stove and bring the sauce to the boil; cook for 2 or 3 minutes. Put the artichokes and the water in which they were boiled through a strainer and blend into the sauce. Taste and adjust the seasoning and bring the soup to simmering point.

**Method.** Cut and trim the meat into 1½ in. cubes and roll in flour. Melt half the fat in a large saucepan or flameproof casserole and brown the meat for a few minutes on each side to seal in the juices. Take the meat out of the pan and keep in a warm place. Melt the remaining fat and fry the onion for 5–10 minutes until it is soft, together with the coconut cream. Add the spices, garlic, tomato paste and salt and cook with the onions for a few minutes. Return the meat to the pan and add the sultanas, nuts, sugar and stock. Bring the stock to boiling point and then either simmer over a low flame or cook in a 'very cool' oven (250F Mark ½) for 2–2½ hours until the meat is tender. If the stock needs further thickening add a little flour, see footnote to beurre manié recipe on page 133. To reheat, bring to boiling point and simmer until the meat has warmed through. Serve with rice and poppadums, pages 120 and 136. In addition provide a selection of the following in separate bowls or on plates; various chutneys, sliced tomato with raw onion rings, sliced banana, sliced green pepper, desiccated coconut, sliced cucumber in french dressing, toasted almonds or peanuts.

**Method.** Skin the peaches and cut them in slices first removing the stone. Lay the peach slices in the bottom of an ovenproof dish or dishes and pour the brandy or sherry over them. Whip the cream until stiff, cover the peaches and place in the refrigerator to chill. **At this point keep the peaches and cream in the refrigerator until the next day.** Cover the cream with a layer of brown sugar between ⅛–¼ in. deep. While the main course is being cleared away place the dish under a preheated hot grill for long enough to caramelize the sugar, but not to completely melt the cream, and serve immediately. The caramelizing process takes 2–3 minutes.

## Gazpacho

*Can be made 1 day ahead   Action time 45 minutes   No cooking*

1¼ pints (3⅛ cups U.S.) bouillon or beef cube

1½ pints (3¾ cups U.S.) tomato juice

¾ lb ripe tomatoes sliced

1 cup (1¼ cups U.S.) Spanish onion finely chopped

12 tablespoons lemon juice

1½ cups (1⅞ cups U.S.) chopped cucumber

9 tablespoons olive oil

9 tablespoons fresh white breadcrumbs

2–3 cloves minced garlic

¾ teaspoon paprika

6 tablespoons tomato paste

few drops tabasco

salt and freshly ground pepper

¼ in. cubes of green pepper and cucumber, also croûtons for garnish, see page 135

## Cold Chicken in Mild Curry Sauce

*Can be made 1 day ahead   Action and cooking time for sauce 30 minutes*

8 cups (10 cups U.S.) chicken (approximately equivalent to two 4½ lb dressed chickens) boiled chicken, page 137

*Sauce*

1½ pints (3¾ cups U.S.) chicken stock*

1½ pints (3¾ cups U.S.) milk

3½ ozs flour

1½ ozs butter

juice of 1 lemon

4½ teaspoons curry powder

¾ pint (1⅞ cups U.S.) soured cream

2 eggs lightly beaten

salt and pepper

½ teaspoon turmeric (optional)

## Chocolate Cherry Gâteau

*Make 1 day ahead   Action time 30 minutes   No cooking*

¾ lb chocolate

1 lb butter

1 lb broken biscuits

4 egg yolks

3 tablespoons golden syrup

4 ozs glacé cherries

4 ozs hazel nuts or walnuts

2 tablespoons rum (optional)

*above* cut legs from body
and remove wing tips

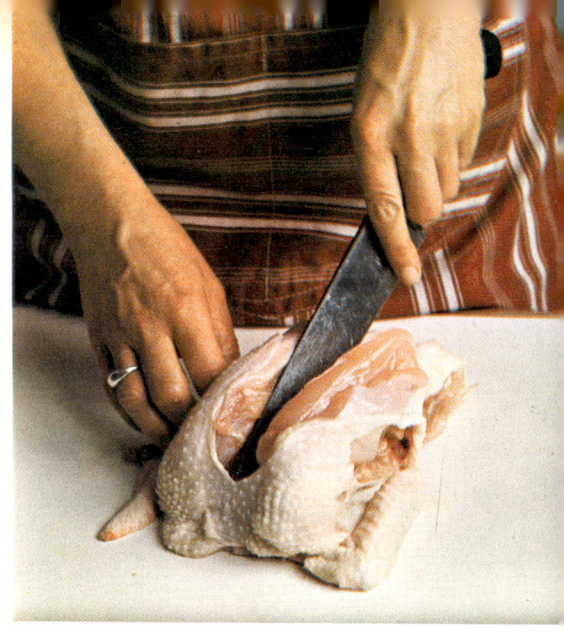

*above* cut breast down
to wing joint, remove wing

JOINTING BIRDS

*below* split back

*below* separated pieces

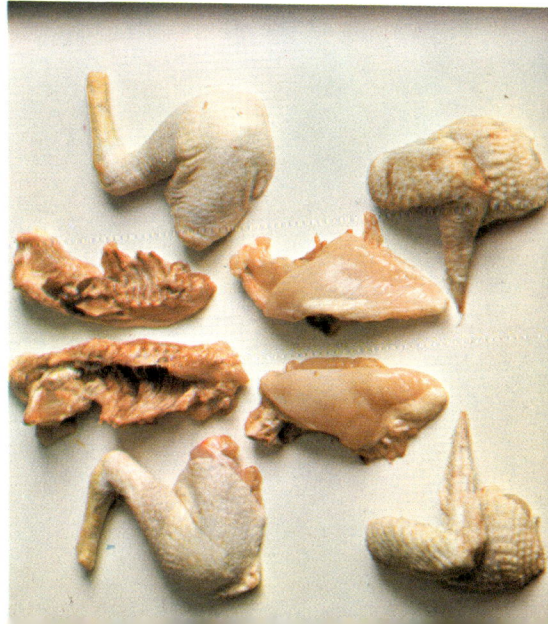

French
Apple
Flan

Ba
Gamm

Tuna Fish
Cannelloni

**Method.** Mix all the ingredients well together in a bowl with the exception of the bouillon, tomato juice and garnish. Leave to marinate for 30 minutes. Add the bouillon and tomato juice and blend in a liquidizer. Taste and adjust the seasoning if necessary. Serve well chilled. Pass round the cubes of pepper and cucumber and the croûtons in separate bowls so that your guests can help themselves.

**Method.** Heat the milk and stock to scalding temperature and remove the pan from the fire. Melt the butter in another saucepan, take from the heat and blend in the flour and curry powder to form a smooth roux. Cook over a low heat until the roux bubbles and begins to turn colour; remove from the fire. Slowly add the stock to the roux stirring as you do so to ensure that the ingredients blend well together. Add the turmeric, return the pan to the fire, and bring the stock to boiling point stirring all the time; reduce the heat and simmer for 2 to 3 minutes. Move the pan from the stove. Add the egg yolks to the sauce together with the lemon, salt and pepper and stir thoroughly. Taste and adjust seasoning if necessary. While the sauce is cooling stir it from time to time to prevent a skin forming or float a piece of butter over the surface. When cold add the soured cream. Spoon the sauce over the chicken just prior to eating. Serve with a choice of salads one of which should be green.

**Method.** Break the chocolate in small pieces and melt it over a pan of simmering water. Melt the butter in a saucepan over a low flame and add the golden syrup; take off the fire and allow to cool slightly. Beat the egg yolks lightly in a large mixing bowl, and slowly pour on the melted butter mixture stirring all the time. Add the melted chocolate and the rum and beat well. Fold in the biscuits, which should first be crushed with a rolling pin. Add the nuts and the cherries keeping a few on one side for decoration. Butter a cake tin with a movable bottom, spoon in the mixture and leave it to set. This cake will cut in firm slices and should be served with pouring cream.

## Smoked Cod Mousse

*Make 1 day ahead   Action and cooking time 45 minutes including 'blender' mayonnaise*

1½ lbs smoked cod*
1 pint (2½ cups U.S.) aspic jelly (Symington's)
½ pint (1¼ cups U.S.) double cream
½ pint (1¼ cups U.S.) egg mayonnaise**
2 tablespoons lemon juice
white pepper
watercress or parsley for decoration

*For a milder flavour use fresh cod, in which case a little salt should be added.
**Hellmann's mayonnaise makes an excellent substitute.


## Terrine of Pork

*Make 1 day ahead   Action time 40 minutes   Cooking time 2¼ hours*

1 lb minced pigs liver
1 lb minced pork
1 lb minced veal
1 lb pork sausage meat
¾ lb bacon rashers
1 medium-sized onion finely chopped
4 tablespoons olive oil

4 tablespoons red wine or sherry
chopped parsley
1 clove garlic minced
2 bay leaves
1 teaspoon basil
¼ teaspoon thyme
salt and pepper

For 6–8 people use half the quantities given above and take 20 minutes off the cooking time.


## Madame Pusich's Iced Pineapple Gâteau

*Make 1 day ahead   Action time 40 minutes   No cooking*

½ lb sponge finger biscuits
2 cans pineapple rings (about 1 lb 13 ozs each)
10 ozs icing sugar
4 eggs
4 tablespoons kirsch or sherry
6 tablespoons apricot jam
½ pint (1¼ cups U.S.) double cream
¾ lb unsalted butter

**Method.** Put the cod in a pan with enough water to almost cover it and poach slowly for about 12 minutes; take from a plan and cool slightly before breaking up with a fork and removing all bones and skin. While the fish is cooking make the aspic jelly. Pour $\frac{1}{4}$ pint of the aspic into a soufflé dish, cool and put in the refrigerator to set. Half-whip the cream. Place the fish and remaining aspic, which should first be cooled to blood temperature, into a blender together with the mayonnaise, cream, lemon juice and pepper and blend thoroughly. Pour the mixture gently on to the firm aspic in the the soufflé dish; allow to set. Turn out by first placing the dish in a bowl of near boiling water for 10–30 seconds; the time depends on the thickness of the dish. Decorate with watercress or parsley and serve with melba toast, page 134, and butter.

**Method.** Line a 5-pint casserole with the bacon rashers having first removed the rind. Mix the liver, veal, salt, pepper, onion, thyme and $\frac{1}{2}$ a teaspoon of basil together in a bowl with 2 tablespoons of oil and 2 of wine or sherry. In a second bowl mix the pork and sausage meat with the rest of the basil, the chopped parsley, the minced garlic and 2 tablespoons of oil and 2 of wine or sherry. Next put the liver mixture in the lined casserole, then the layer of pork and lastly the bay leaves. Put the lid on the casserole and place it in a pan filled with boiling water and cook in a 'cool to warm' oven (300–325F Mark 2–3) for 2 hours 15 minutes. When the cooking time is up, take the terrine out of the oven and remove the lid and the bay leaves. Cover the terrine with foil and sit a heavy weight on it – heavy pots of jam are useful for this purpose. Keep in a cool place for at least 24 hours. To ease the job of turning out the terrine, stand the casserole in a bowl of near boiling water for about 1 minute and run a knife between the bacon and the dish.

**Method.** Drain as much juice as possible from the pineapple slices; keep 8 rings whole for decoration and cut the remaining rings into small pieces. Break $\frac{1}{2}$ lb of sponge finger biscuits into $\frac{3}{4}$ in. length pieces and put them into a bowl and add the kirsch or sherry. Next cream the butter and icing sugar together until soft and smooth. Separate the yolks from the whites of the egg and lightly beat the yolks. Blend the yolks into the creamed butter and sugar, add the pineapple pieces and sponge finger biscuits and mix thoroughly. Beat the cream until stiff and also the whites of egg. Fold the cream into the pineapple mixture and then fold in the white of egg. Divide the mixture equally between two buttered 7 in. flan or cake tins with movable bottoms; cover the cakes with foil and leave to set in the ice making compartment of the refrigerator for at least 12 hours. About 1 hour before serving, remove the cakes to plates with the help of a palate knife. Place 4 rings of pineapple on top of each and fill the centres with apricot jam. Do not refreeze but keep cool in the refrigerator as this gâteau should be eaten when it is part-frozen.

# Fork Supper for 16

### Pâté Maison

*Make 1 day ahead    Action time 30 minutes    Cooking time 2½ hours*

1 lb minced pork
1 lb minced veal
2 lbs minced pigs liver
¾ lb bacon rashers
4 cloves garlic, minced or pounded
¼ teaspoon sage
¼ teaspoon thyme
2 tablespoons brandy

2 teaspoons salt
Flour for sealing pâté jar or casserole
*Marinade*
6 tablespoons red wine
2 tablespoons oil
2 medium-sized onions finely chopped
freshly ground pepper
2 bay leaves

For 8 people use half the above, except for the bacon where you will need ½ lb. Cook for 2 hours.

### Chicken and Almonds in Lemon Sauce

*Can be made 1 day ahead    Action and cooking time for sauce 30 minutes*

8 cups (10 cups U.S.) chicken
  (approximately equivalent to two
  4½ lb dressed chickens)
boiled chicken, page 137
*Sauce*
1½ pints (3¾ cups U.S.) chicken stock
1½ pints (3¾ cups U.S.) milk
juice and grated rind of 2 lemons

4½ ozs flour
3 ozs butter
2 egg yolks lightly beaten
¼ lb almonds
½ pint (1¼ cups U.S.) double cream
1 teaspoon salt
white pepper

### Lychee and Black Grape Salad

*Can be prepared 1 day ahead    Action time 40 minutes    Cooking time 15 minutes*

2½ lbs lychees
1¼ lbs black grapes
6 tablespoons sugar
1¼ pints (3⅛ cups U.S.) water
⅜ pint (1 5/16 cup U.S.) strong china tea*
juice of 1 lemon
2 teaspoons arrowroot

*See note on page 52.
If you buy canned lychees use the syrup in the tin and add the lemon juice and china tea.

84

**Method.** To form the marinade mix the red wine, oil, onion, bay leaves and pepper together. Stand the minced pork, liver and veal in this mixture for about 3 hours and turn once or twice during that time. Line a pâté jar or casserole with the bacon having first removed the rind. Add the brandy, the garlic, herbs, and salt to the minced meat in the marinade; stir well and extract the bay leaves before placing the meat in the bacon-lined dish. Seal the lid with a flour and water paste to ensure that no moisture escapes. Sit the dish in a pan of boiling water and cook in a 'cool to warm' oven for 2–2½ hours (300–325F Mark 2–3). Take the dish out of the oven and remove the lid. Cover the pâté with foil, sit a heavy weight on top, a heavy tin of syrup or jar of jam will do, and keep it in a refrigerator or cool place for 24 hours before turning out.

**Method.** First blanch the almonds to remove the skin and then bake them in a 'cool' oven (300F Mark 2) for 15 minutes. To make the sauce, heat the milk and stock to scalding temperature in a saucepan and remove from the fire. Melt the butter slowly in another pan, take away from the heat and stir in the flour until the roux is smooth. Cook over a low heat until the roux bubbles and begins to turn colour; remove from the fire. Add the scalded stock stirring all the time so that the ingredients blend well together. Return the pan to the heat and continue stirring until the mixture thickens. Add the lemon juice and rind, salt and pepper and cook for a further 3–4 minutes. Put the chicken and almonds in the sauce and heat slowly for 10–15 minutes. **At this point the chicken and sauce can be kept until the next day and then be brought to simmering point over a low flame.** Just before serving stir in the egg yolks and the cream; do not allow to boil. Serve with lettuce and chicory salad and plain boiled rice; allow 2 ozs rice per person.
If you are reheating this sauce it may be necessary to thin it with a little stock as it should be thin, though not so thin that it runs straight through the rice.

**Method.** Put the water and sugar together in a saucepan and bring slowly to the boil; simmer for 10 minutes. Mix the arrowroot with 1 tablespoon of water in a bowl and pour over the sugar syrup stirring all the time. Transfer the contents of the bowl back to the saucepan; add the tea and lemon juice and cook for a few minutes until the syrup thickens. Remove from the fire and cool. Skin the lychees and either cut them in half or slit them down the side to remove the stone. Cut the grapes in half and remove the seeds. Since the charm of this combination of fruits is the contrast between the white lychees and black grapes, do not remove the grape skins unless they are particularly tough. **The syrup, the lychees and grapes can be kept in covered containers in the refrigerator overnight.** Pour the syrup over the fruit an hour or two before serving and chill.

# Menus for the Unexpected Guest
(*All these recipes serve 4*)

Store Cupboard                                            88

**First Courses**                                  *page*  89
Taramasalata
Consommé with Egg and Parmesan Cheese                     89
Soufflé Oeuf en Cocotte                                   89
Herrings in Soured Cream                                  90
Mock Bisque                                               90

**Main Courses**
Kedgeree                                                  91
Omelette Arnold Bennett                                   91
Tuna Fish Cannelloni                                      92
Ham and Pimento Kebabs                                    92
Lasagne                                                   93
Chinese Risotto                                           93
Eggs Benedict                                             94
Egg and Bacon Pie                                         94
Chilli Con Carne                                          95

**Puddings**
Queen's Peaches                                           95
Pancakes                                                  96
Damsons Baked with Bread                                  96
Apple with Ground Almonds                                 96
Zabaione                                                  97
Pears with Chocolate Sauce                                97

To people who are fond of eating the term 'convenience foods' has an unattractive ring. Meat and vegetables are not on the whole improved by being tinned, and fish such as salmon, tuna fish and sardines take on entirely new flavours, though special brands of sardines are treated as a delicacy by many gourmets. Nonetheless, the following pages are devoted to appetizing dishes made from tinned and store-cupboard foods. Incidentally the quantities required for fresh meat and fish are also given. With a well-stocked store cupboard it is possible to issue invitations on the spur of the moment, knowing that the food can be something more interesting than eggs and bacon or a plain omelette. It is perhaps also worth mentioning that several of the dishes are suitable for sailing and camping holidays, and Chinese risotto, kedgeree, chilli con carne and mock bisque can be specially recommended when only one or two burners are available. As an unexpected guest is likely to think himself lucky to be given even two courses, no attempt has been made to set the dishes out in the form of menus.

The lists which follow contain all the ingredients which are used in the 'unexpected guest' recipes plus a few basic additions.

## Basic Foods

Arrowroot
Aspic jelly
Bacon*
Butter*
Bread
Cheese – parmesan and cheddar or
  gruyère
Eggs
Flour
Garlic
Gelatine
Herbs and spices
Lard*
Lemon juice
Milk – dried
Mustard – French and English
Oil – cooking and olive
Onions
Pepper
Salt
Stock cubes – beef and chicken
Sugar – castor and demerara
Tomato paste

## Jars

Smoked cod's roe*
Marinated herrings

## Miscellaneous

Chocolate – cooking or plain dessert
Ground almonds
Peanuts
Soy sauce
Soured cream*†
Surprise peas
Walnuts

*Should be kept in a refrigerator.
†See page 90

## Packet Mixes

Shortcrust pastry
Sauces – white
       – cheese

## Pasta and Rice

Lasagne
Noodles
Rice

## Tinned Foods

*Fish*
Salmon
Shrimps
Smoked haddock
Tuna

*Fruit*
Apples – stewed
Damsons
Peach halves
Pears
Pineapple slices

*Meat*
Ham
Minced Beef
Pâté

*Vegetables*
Carrots
Kidney beans
Mushrooms
Petits pois
Potatoes
Red pimentos
Tomatoes

## Wines

Marsala
Sherry

**Taramasalata**

*Action time 10 minutes   No cooking*

1 jar smoked cod's roe (about 3½ ozs)
juice of ½ a lemon
2 tablespoons olive oil
3 ozs butter
3 tablespoons fresh white breadcrumbs
chopped chives for garnish (if available)

Pound the smoked cod's roe, blend in the butter and then the other ingredients. Put in a bowl and decorate with chopped chives. Serve with toast and butter.
(For recipe for fresh smoked cod's roe, see page 66)

**Consommé with Egg and Parmesan Cheese**

*Action and cooking time 15 minutes*

2 tins (about 10½ ozs) beef consommé
1 slice toasted bread
4 eggs
2 tablespoons grated parmesan cheese

Open the tins and heat the consommé in a saucepan. Meanwhile have ready the slice of toast cut in four with the crusts removed. Sit the pieces of toast in individual soup cups which have first been well warmed. Break the eggs on to the toast and pour the soup over them taking great care not to break the yolks. Serve with the parmesan cheese scattered over the surface of the soup. If you do not like the idea of semi-raw eggs these can first be poached in the consommé, in which case it will be necessary to pour the soup into the bowls through a strainer to catch any egg white which may be floating in it.

**Soufflé Oeufs en Cocotte**

*Action time 10 minutes   Cooking time 10 minutes*

4 eggs
2 rashers bacon cut in ½ in. squares or small pieces of ham
3 tablespoons grated cheddar cheese
salt and freshly ground pepper

Gently sauté the bacon, and divide the bacon or ham equally between 4 buttered ramekin dishes; these preferably should have a 3 in. diameter. Separate the whites from the yolks of egg taking great care not to break the latter, which should be put on one side in individual containers. Whisk the whites of egg until they are stiff and add the salt and pepper. Spoon the whites of egg into the ramekins and mould a slight hollow in the centre of each one. Place a yolk of egg in each hollow, sprinkle over a little grated cheese and put the ramekins in a pan containing water which has recently boiled. Cook in a 'moderate to fairly hot' oven (350–375F Mark 4–5) for about 10 minutes.


## Herrings in Soured Cream

*Action time 5 minutes    No cooking*

    1 jar marinated herring fillets* (about 12 ozs)
    $\frac{1}{4}$ pint ($\frac{5}{8}$ cup U.S.) soured cream
    paprika

Open the jar of herring fillets and drain off the liquid from the onion and fish. Place the herrings and the onion on a dish and pour over the soured cream. Sprinkle with paprika for decoration.

If it is fresh when bought soured cream will keep for 2–3 weeks in a refrigerator.
*Sometimes these are sold rolled.


## Mock Bisque

*Action time 10 minutes    Cooking time 15 minutes*

    1 tin condensed tomato soup (about $11\frac{1}{4}$ ozs)
    1 tin condensed green pea soup (about $11\frac{1}{4}$ ozs)
    3 tablespoons sherry
    $\frac{3}{4}$ pint ($1\frac{7}{8}$ cups U.S.) milk
    1 small tin shrimps (optional)

Open the cans and heat the tomato and green pea soup together in a saucepan until they reach boiling point. Remove the pan from the stove and add the milk. Return the pan to the fire and heat taking great care to see that the soup does not boil. Just before serving add the sherry and the shrimps. Make croûtons, see page 151.
The combination of these two soups produces a faint flavour of shellfish; the addition of a few shrimps adds greatly to the illusion.

## Kedgeree

*Action time 10 minutes    Cooking time 25 minutes*

1 tin salmon (about 8 ozs)
3 hard-boiled eggs
½ lb rice
4 ozs butter
parsley finely chopped (if available)
salt and freshly ground pepper

Wash the rice and cook it in boiling water for about 15–20 minutes; remove from the fire, strain and rinse under running water to remove any excess starch. Meanwhile open the tin of salmon and drain off all the liquid. Chop the hard-boiled eggs. Melt the butter in a saucepan and add the fish, rice, salt and pepper and heat together for 3 to 4 minutes gently stirring all the time. Just before serving add the hard-boiled egg and parsley.
If making with fresh fish use ½ lb of cooked smoked cod and ½ lb of cooked fresh haddock.

## Omelette Arnold Bennett

*Action and cooking time 20 minutes*

6 eggs
1 tin smoked haddock (about 7½ ozs)
packet of white sauce mix
½ pint (1¼ cups U.S.) milk
¼ lb grated gruyère or cheddar cheese
1 oz butter
salt and pepper

Open the tin of smoked haddock and drain off all the liquid. Remove the skin and flake the fish with a fork. Make the white sauce. Break the eggs in a bowl and add 2 tablespoonsful of water together with salt and pepper. Beat the eggs with a fork for about 30 seconds and then mix in the fish. Melt the butter in an omelette pan, preferably one with a 10 in. diameter, and when the butter is hot and foaming pour on the egg mixture; stir once or twice with the flat of the fork. As the omelette begins to set carefully lift the sides to allow the uncooked egg to run through and shake the pan from side to side to keep the omelette from sticking. Pre-heat the grill. When the omelette is cooked, but still soft on top, cover the surface evenly with the

91

white sauce and sprinkle with the cheese. Grill until light brown. For fresh fish use $\frac{1}{4}$–$\frac{1}{2}$ lb cooked smoked haddock and make the white sauce with single cream. Eat with a green salad.


## Tuna Fish Cannelloni

*Action and cooking time 35 minutes*

| | |
|---|---|
| 1 tin tuna fish (about 8 ozs) | squeeze of tomato paste |
| 6 sheets lasagne* | 1 tablespoon cooking oil |
| 2 packets cheese sauce mix | pinch of mace |
| 1 pint (2$\frac{1}{2}$ cups U.S.) milk | salt |
| 4 tablespoons grated cheese | freshly ground pepper |
| 1 teaspoon grated onion | |

*Now obtainable in many stores and supermarkets.

Boil the lasagne for 20 minutes in salted water, to which has been added 1 tablespoon of cooking oil. Make 1 pint of cheese sauce according to the instructions on the packet. Open the tin of tuna fish and drain off the liquid. Flake the tuna fish with a fork and put it in a saucepan; add half the cheese sauce, a squeeze of tomato paste, the onion, mace, salt and pepper. Heat the tuna fish mixture through and keep hot over a low flame until the lasagne is ready. Drain the water from the lasagne and lay the sheets out on a board. Place a little of the tuna fish mixture in a strip down the centre of each one and fold the sides over. Move to a shallow fireproof dish with the aid of a fish slice. Cover the rest of the cheese sauce, sprinkle over the grated cheese and brown under a hot grill for 3 or 4 minutes before serving.


## Ham and Pimento Kebabs

*Action and cooking time 25 minutes*

| | |
|---|---|
| 1 tin ham (about 1 lb) | freshly ground pepper |
| 1 tin red pimentos (about 4$\frac{1}{2}$ ozs) | $\frac{1}{2}$ lb rice |
| 1 tin pineapple rings (about 15 ozs) | 1 teaspoon turmeric |
| 8 bay leaves | salt |
| 2 ozs butter | |

Remove the ham from the tin and cut it in 1 inch cubes. Open the tins of pimento and pineapple, cut each pimento in four and each pineapple ring in three. Put the pieces of ham on skewers alternating with pieces of pimento, pineapple and bay leaves. Dot with knobs of butter, sprinkle with freshly ground pepper, and grill for 4 minutes on each side. Serve on a bed of rice. Add salt to the water in which the rice is cooked, also turmeric to make the rice yellow and to give it a faint aromatic flavour.

## Lasagne

*Action time 20 minutes    Cooking time 40 minutes*

| | |
|---|---|
| 1 tin minced beef (about 15 ozs) | 3 tablespoons tomato paste |
| 8 sheets lasagne* | 1 tablespoon cooking oil |
| 2 packets cheese sauce mix | 2 tablespoons grated parmesan cheese |
| 1 pint (2½ cups U.S.) milk | salt and pepper |

*Now obtainable in many stores and supermarkets.

Fill a large saucepan with water, add salt and 1 tablespoon of cooking oil and bring the water to the boil. Cook the sheets of lasagne in the water for 20 minutes. Meanwhile make the sauce according to the instructions on the packet. Open the tin of meat and heat up the contents, add the tomato paste and season with salt and pepper. Take the saucepan containing the lasagne off the fire, pour away the water and drain the lasagne. As soon as they are cool enough to touch separate the sheets and line the bottom of a fireproof dish. Pour over a little of the meat, then the sauce and then a layer of lasagne. Repeat this process several times and finish with a layer of sauce. Sprinkle the cheese over the sauce and bake in a 'moderate' oven (350F Mark 4) for 20 minutes.

When making this dish with fresh meat start by gently frying a small finely chopped onion, add ¾ lb minced meat, 2 sliced tomatoes and salt and pepper and cook for about 10 minutes.

## Chinese Risotto

*Action and cooking time 35 minutes*

| | |
|---|---|
| 6 rashers bacon | 1 tablespoon soy sauce |
| 2 eggs | 1 large onion finely chopped |
| ½ lb patna rice | 2 tablespoons olive oil |
| 2 ozs sultanas | 1 oz butter |
| 2 ozs salted peanuts | salt and pepper |

Cook the rice for 10–15 minutes in fast-boiling water, rinse, drain thoroughly and dry in a cool oven while the rest of the ingredients are being prepared. Meanwhile heat the oil in a pan and gently fry the onion for about 5 minutes. Cut the bacon in inch-length pieces and add to the onion in the pan; continue cooking for another 10 minutes. Make an omelette; break the eggs into a bowl and beat them lightly with a fork, add 1 tablespoonful of water and salt and pepper. Melt the butter in a small omelette pan and when it starts to foam pour on the egg. Once the egg starts to set lift up the edge to allow the uncooked egg to run through and shake the pan back and forth to prevent the omelette sticking to the pan. When still soft on top cut the omelette into 1 in. squares. Put the omelette, nuts, sultanas, soy sauce and rice in the pan with the onion and bacon and mix all the ingredients gently together with a fork.

## Eggs Benedict

*Action and cooking time 30 minutes*

| | |
|---|---|
| 4 eggs | *Hollandaise sauce*\* |
| $\frac{1}{4}$ lb thinly sliced fresh or tinned ham | 3 egg yolks |
| 4 slices bread | $\frac{1}{2}$ lb butter |
| | 2 tablespoons lemon juice |
| \*Use quick blender method. | salt and freshly ground pepper |

Cut the bread in circular shapes. Put the butter in a saucepan and melt it slowly. Meanwhile poach the eggs, see page 138, grill the ham and toast the bread. Put the egg yolks, lemon juice, salt and pepper in a blender and switch the motor to high for 3 or 4 seconds. Turn the heat up until the butter in the saucepan bubbles. Switch the motor again to high on the blender, and ease the lid to one side to make room to pour on the butter slowly in a steady stream. By the time the saucepan is empty the sauce should be ready. Divide the ham equally between the four rounds of bread and place a poached egg on top of each piece. Cover with the hollandaise sauce and serve immediately.

## Egg and Bacon Pie

*Action time 30 minutes    Cooking time 35 minutes*

| | |
|---|---|
| Short crust pastry mix ($\frac{1}{2}$ lb) | $\frac{1}{4}$ lb grated cheddar cheese |
| packet white sauce mix | $\frac{1}{4}$ lb bacon |
| $\frac{1}{2}$ pint ($1\frac{1}{4}$ cups U.S.) milk | 1 oz butter |
| 2 eggs | freshly ground pepper |

Make the pastry according to the instructions on the packet. Roll it out on a floured board and line a buttered 8 in. flan dish with a movable bottom. Grill the bacon and cut it into $\frac{1}{2}$ in. strips. Beat the eggs lightly together in a bowl. Blend the white sauce mix with the milk in a saucepan and stirring all the time bring slowly to the boil. Remove from the fire and stir in the eggs, bacon and $\frac{3}{4}$ of the cheese; season with freshly ground pepper. Pour the mixture into the flan case, sprinkle over the rest of the cheese and dot with knobs of butter. Cook in a 'hot' oven (425F Mark 7) for 35 minutes. Remove from the flan case and cool slightly before serving.

## Chilli Con Carne

*Action time 10 minutes    Cooking time 15 minutes*

1 tin tomatoes (about 15 ozs)
1 tin red kidney beans (about 11 ozs)
1 tin minced beef (about 15 ozs)
1 onion finely chopped
2 tablespoons cooking oil

1 clove garlic minced or pounded
$\frac{1}{8}$–$\frac{1}{4}$ teaspoon chilli powder

Fry the onions in oil until transparent. Add the rest of the ingredients and cook for 10–15 minutes. Although traditionally eaten on its own, chilli con carne can be served with either rice, spaghetti or noodles.

## Queen's Peaches

*Action time 10 minutes    Cooking time 15 minutes*

1 tin peach halves (about 15 ozs)
2 whites of egg
8 tablespoons castor sugar
grated peel of 1 lemon or a little lemon juice
walnuts

Beat the white of egg until stiff and fold in the sugar. Put a little grated peel or lemon juice in the hollow of each peach and top with a spoonful of the beaten white of egg and a walnut. Place the peaches together with their juice in an ovenproof dish and bake in a 'moderate' oven (350F Mark 4) for 15 minutes.

## Pancakes

*Action time including making batter 30 minutes    Cooking time 20 minutes*

½ pint (1¼ cups U.S.) batter, page 136
2 ozs butter
1 lemon or lemon juice
castor sugar

Melt a piece of butter, about the size of a nut, in a frying pan. When the fat is hot and a faint haze rising from the pan pour in a little batter, just enough to thinly cover the bottom of the pan. Once the batter has set shake the pan to prevent it sticking to the bottom; cook until brown and then toss or turn the pancake over and brown on the other side. When brown on both sides lift the pancake from the pan sprinkle over white sugar and fold in three. Cover and keep in a low oven while the other pancakes are being cooked. Serve with quarters of lemon or lemon juice and more sugar.

## Damsons Baked with Bread

*Action time 15 minutes    Cooking time 20 minutes*

1 tin damsons (about 15 ozs)
2 thick slices of bread
3 tablespoons demerara sugar
squeeze of lemon juice
1 oz butter

Butter a shallow fireproof dish. Cut the crusts off the bread and line the dish. Open the tin of damsons and strain the fruit from the juice. Remove the stones from the damsons. Arrange the fruit on the bread, add a squeeze of lemon juice, cover with brown sugar and dot with knobs of butter. Bake in a 'moderate' oven (350F Mark 4) for 20 minutes. Heat the juice and serve it separately in a jug.

## Apple with Ground Almonds

*Action time 15 minutes    Cooking time 20 minutes*

| | |
|---|---|
| 1 tin stewed apple (about 15 ozs) | 2 ozs sugar |
| 2 ozs ground almonds | 1 egg yolk |
| 2 ozs butter | |

Open the tin and divide the apples between 4 ramekin dishes, preferably with a 3 in. diameter. Cream the butter and sugar together in a bowl and add the egg and almonds to form a paste. Roll the paste out on a floured board and cut in 4 rings about ⅓ in. thick. Cover the apples with the rings of paste and bake in a 'moderate' oven (350F Mark 4) for 20 minutes.
(1 lb freshly stewed apples can be used instead of the tinned apple.)

## Zabaione

*Action and cooking time 10 minutes*

    6 egg yolks
    6 tablespoons castor sugar
    6 tablespoons marsala

With an egg beater whisk the egg yolks and sugar together in a double-boiler or in a basin over simmering water for about 3 minutes. Add the marsala and continue whisking for about another 5 minutes, until the mixture rises and becomes thick and frothy. Pour into warmed glasses with sugared rims and serve at once.

## Pears with Chocolate Sauce

*Action and cooking time including sauce 10 minutes*

    1 tin (about 15 ozs) pears
    ½ pint (1¼ cups U.S.) chocolate sauce

Make the chocolate sauce on page 130 and allow to cool. Open the tin of pears and strain off all the juice. Place the pears, curved side uppermost, in a glass dish and spoon over the chocolate sauce. If possible chill before serving.

# Ideas for Drinks Parties

| | | |
|---|---|---|
| Avocado Dip | *page* | 100 |
| Tuna Fish Dip | | 100 |
| Cauliflower Dip | | 100 |
| Artichoke Leaves with Prawns | | 101 |
| Quick Chicken Liver Pâté | | 101 |
| Double-decker Sandwiches | | 102 |
| Onion Puffs | | 102 |
| Nut Cheese Balls | | 103 |
| Salted Almond Sandwiches | | 103 |
| Devilled Peanuts | | 103 |
| Stuffed Dates and Grapes | | 104 |
| Pastry Petits Fours | | 104 |
| Ham and Asparagus Squares | | 105 |
| Mushroom and Shrimp Vol-au-vents | | 105 |
| Sausage Pastry Rings | | 106 |
| Sausage Balls | | 106 |
| Prune and Bacon Rolls | | 107 |
| Kidney and Bacon Rolls | | 107 |
| Stuffed Celery | | 108 |

Eats with drinks can either be of the small mouth-sized variety or they can be more substantial. The latter is a good idea if the drinks take place before a theatre, or some other event which means a long delay before the next meal. For a drinks party it is a mistake to make too many different things, particularly if you are doing the catering single-handed, as they are time-consuming to prepare. A dip, two kinds of canapés and something hot is quite sufficient for the average party; allow 4 to 5 eats per person. If you wish to give your guests something more substantial, choose from one or two of the following; taramasalata, or liver, fish, buckling or kipper pâté. These can be eaten with pumpernickel, or toast and butter. Make the table look attractive by setting out plates of olives and radishes, and also provide sticks of celery or a bowl of watercress.

## Avocado Dip

*Action time 10 minutes    No cooking*

1 avocado pear
juice of $\frac{1}{2}$ a lemon
$\frac{1}{4}$ lb cream cheese
a few drops tabasco
salt

Peel the avocado pear and remove the stone. Put the avocado together with the other ingredients in a blender and pulverize thoroughly. This dip can be made without the use of an electric blender by crushing the avocado well with a fork and slowly blending in the cream cheese and other ingredients. Eat with small biscuits, crisps or carrot sticks.

## Tuna Fish Dip

*Can be made 1 day ahead    Action time 10 minutes    No cooking*

1 tin tuna fish (about 4 ozs)
$\frac{1}{2}$ pint (1$\frac{1}{4}$ cups U.S.) soured cream
$\frac{1}{4}$ lb cream cheese
1 clove garlic
few drops tabasco
salt
$\frac{1}{4}$ lb shrimps (optional)

Break the tuna fish up with a fork. Blend in the cream cheese followed by the soured cream. Add the minced garlic, tabasco and a little salt. Decorate with shrimps and eat with small cheese biscuits, crisps or carrot sticks.

## Cauliflower Dip

*Can be made 1 day ahead    Action time 15 minutes    No cooking*

| | |
|---|---|
| 1 cauliflower | $\frac{1}{2}$ lb Danish blue cheese |
| *Dip* | squeeze of tomato paste |
| $\frac{1}{2}$ pint (1$\frac{1}{4}$ cups U.S.) soured cream | $\frac{1}{2}$ teaspoon paprika |

Break up the cheese with a fork and slowly blend in the soured cream; add the paprika and tomato paste. Wash the cauliflower and cut the white flower, with a short stalk attached, into small pieces suitable for eating in one or two mouthfuls. For serving, place the dip in a bowl and sit this in either a large bowl or on a board with the cauliflower surrounding it.

### Artichoke Leaves with Prawns

*Action time about 25 minutes    No cooking*

    1 medium-sized artichoke (about 45 leaves)
    4 ozs prawns
    1 tablespoon Philadelphia cream cheese
    2 tablespoons egg mayonnaise, page 127
    a few drops tabasco
    squeeze of tomato paste

Cook the artichoke by steaming it for 35 minutes. Meanwhile mix the cream cheese, mayonnaise, tabasco and tomato paste together. Remove the artichoke from the heat and allow to get cold. Strip the leaves off and place a little of the cream cheese mixture together with a prawn on the edible part near the base of each leaf.
The centre of the artichoke can be chopped, mixed with a little mayonnaise and used as a filling for petits fours cases, see page 104. Add colour by sprinkling with paprika.

### Quick Chicken Liver Pâté

*Can be made 1 day ahead    Action and cooking time 20 minutes*

    $\frac{1}{2}$ lb chicken livers
    $\frac{1}{4}$ lb mushrooms
    $\frac{1}{4}$ lb butter
    1 clove minced garlic (optional)
    salt and freshly ground pepper

Wash the mushrooms; fry the chicken livers in a little of the butter for 6 or 7 minutes. Melt the rest of the butter in another saucepan; put this together with the cooked chicken liver, raw mushrooms and their stalks, salt, pepper and garlic in a blender. Blend until thoroughly smooth, pour into a small soufflé dish and leave to set.
For a drinks party this pâté can be used on inch squares of toast or fried bread, and decorated with parsley or paprika. It can also be used as a first course for lunch or dinner, in which case it should be served with toast and butter.

## Double-decker Sandwiches

*Make 1 day ahead    Action time 35 minutes*

3 ozs liver pâté* see page 101
2 ozs butter
1 oz Danish blue cheese
parsley or paprika for decoration
1 oz cream cheese
4 slices bread

*Pâté parfait in a tin will do as an alternative.
The above recipe makes about 36 canapés.

Blend the Danish blue cheese with the cream cheese, and in another bowl blend the pâté with the butter. Spread 2 slices of bread thickly with the pâté paste and 1 slice with the cheese paste. Place the pâté and cheese slices in alternate layers to form a sandwich and top with the fourth slice of bread. Press the slices firmly together and wrap them tightly in foil. Keep in the ice making compartment of the refrigerator for at least 5 hours. While still frozen cut the crusts of the bread; then cutting downwards divide the sandwich into three and cut again at ¼ in. intervals to form small canapés. Before serving, allow about 30 minutes for the canapés to unfreeze. These can be decorated with finely chopped parsley or paprikia.
Various fillings can be used for these canapés; anchovy butter with avocado and cream cheese paste is one of many alternatives. The important thing is to remember that all fillings must be of the paste variety otherwise the canapés will fall apart once they unfreeze.

## Onion Puffs

*Action time 15 minutes    Cooking time 15 minutes*

3 teaspoons onion finely chopped
4 slices white bread
4 tablespoons Hellmann's mayonnaise

The above ingredients are sufficient for 24 onion puffs.

Remove the crusts from the bread and cut the slices into 1 in. squares. Place a little chopped onion on each bread square and cover it with half a teaspoon of mayonnaise. Bake in a 'hot' oven (425F Mark 7) for about 15 minutes. Serve hot.

## Nut Cheese Balls

*Can be made 1 day ahead    Action time 30 minutes    No cooking*

$\frac{1}{4}$ lb grated cheddar cheese

1 packet Philadelphia cream cheese (3 ozs)

pinch of chilli powder

$\frac{1}{2}$ teaspoon Worcestershire sauce

$\frac{1}{4}$ cup chopped walnuts

The above makes approximately 24 nut cheese balls.

Mix the cheddar cheese and cream cheese together with the chilli powder and Worcestershire sauce. Shape into balls about the size of small grapes and roll in the nuts; chill.

## Salted Almond Sandwiches

*Action and cooking time 20 minutes*

$\frac{1}{4}$ lb almonds

6 slices brown bread

2 oz butter

salt

The above ingredients make about 18 small sandwiches.

First blanch the almonds, then melt half the butter in a frying pan and sauté the almonds until they become well browned. Take the almonds out of the pan and roll them in salt. Butter the bread, spread 3 of the slices with salted almonds and cover with the 3 remaining slices to form sandwiches. Trim off the crusts and cut in $1-1\frac{1}{2}$ in. squares.

## Devilled Peanuts

*Action and cooking time 5 minutes*

$\frac{1}{4}$ lb salted peanuts

1 oz butter

2 teaspoons curry powder

Melt the butter, add the curry powder and cook for 1 minute. Fry the peanuts in this mixture for 2 or 3 minutes. Remove the peanuts from the pan and drain them on a piece of absorbent paper. Serve cold.

## Stuffed Dates and Grapes

*Can be made 1 day ahead    Action time 35 minutes    No cooking*

24 dates

$\frac{1}{2}$ lb grapes (about 36 grapes)

60 blanched almonds (about 4 ozs)

2 packets Philadelphia cream cheese (about 3 ozs each)

Remove the stones from the dates and the seeds from the grapes, taking care to see that the halves of the fruit are still held together by a little skin. Stuff with cream cheese and decorate with blanched almonds. Prunes can also be stuffed with cream cheese but these should first be soaked in water for 6 hours.

## Pastry Petits Fours

*Pastry petits fours cases and fillings can be prepared 1 day ahead*
*Action and cooking time about 2 hours*

Pastry petits fours can be filled with a wide range of ingredients with bases of either mayonnaise or béchamel. Petits fours baking tins can be obtained from Leon Jaegi, 232, Tottenham Court Road, London W.1.

*Pastry petits fours cases*
$\frac{1}{2}$ lb short crust pastry, see page 149 makes approximately 7–8 dozen cases

Roll out the pastry to the thickness of $\frac{1}{16}$ to $\frac{1}{8}$ inch and line the petits fours tins. Bake blind in a 'hot' oven (425F Mark 7) for about 17 minutes. Remove from the tins and place on a wire rack to cool. Store in an airtight container until ready to use.

*Egg and anchovy filling*

2 hard-boiled eggs

2 tablespoons mayonnaise, see page 127

$\frac{1}{2}$ teaspoon anchovy essence

pinch of salt

freshly ground pepper

parsley or paprika for decoration

The above ingredients are enough for about 3–3$\frac{1}{2}$ dozen cases.

Chop the hard-boiled egg in small pieces and mix it with the mayonnaise, anchovy essence, salt and freshly ground pepper. Spoon this mixture into the pastry cases and decorate either with chopped parsley or sprinkle with paprika.

*Lemon and mushroom filling*

$\frac{1}{4}$ lb mushrooms thinly sliced

1 tablespoon lemon juice

1 tablespoon water

1 oz butter

$\frac{1}{8}$ pint ($\frac{5}{16}$ cup U.S.) single cream

1–2 tablespoons beurre manié

salt and freshly ground pepper

The above ingredients are enough for about 3–3$\frac{1}{2}$ dozen cases.

Melt the butter in a saucepan and add the water, lemon juice, salt and pepper. Slowly simmer the mushrooms in this mixture for about 5 minutes or until they are tender. Add the beurre manié and cook for 2 to 3 minutes; just before removing from the stove add the cream. Cool before spooning into the pastry cases.

## Ham and Asparagus Squares

*Action time 30 minutes   No cooking*

$\frac{1}{4}$ lb ham thinly sliced
7 slices white bread
1 small tin asparagus

$\frac{1}{2}$ pint (1$\frac{1}{4}$ cups U.S.) Symington's aspic jelly
$\frac{1}{2}$ oz butter

The above ingredients are sufficient for about 42 squares.

First make the aspic according to the instructions on the packet and leave to cool. Remove the crusts from the bread, lightly butter it and cover with the ham. Then with a sharp knife mark out 1–1$\frac{1}{2}$ in. squares on the ham and place a small piece of asparagus in the centre of each. Arrange the slices of bread with the sides touching in a baking tin; when the aspic has reached the point where it is starting to set spoon it over the slices of bread covering them to a thickness of about $\frac{1}{8}$ of an inch. **If you leave the aspic too long it can always be reheated and the cooling process repeated.** Once the aspic has set remove the ham slices from the baking tray, trim the edges and cut into squares.

Wrap slices of thin buttered bread round any remaining asparagus, squeeze firmly and cut at 1$\frac{1}{2}$ in. intervals to form asparagus rolls.

## Mushroom and Shrimp Vol-au-vents

*Vol-au-vent cases can be made 1 day ahead   Action time about 1 hour*
*Cooking time 30 minutes*

*Vol-au-vent cases*
$\frac{1}{2}$ lb puff pastry,* page 133
*Mushroom and shrimp filling*
2 ozs mushrooms thinly sliced
2 ozs shrimps

$\frac{1}{4}$ pint ($\frac{5}{8}$ cup U.S.) béchamel sauce page 123
2 teaspoons sherry
$\frac{1}{2}$ oz butter
salt and freshly ground pepper

The above ingredients are enough for 24 cases.
*Frozen pastry can be used.

105

*Vol-au-vent cases:* flour a pastry board and roll the pastry out to a thickness of about $\frac{1}{4}$ inch. Cut the pastry into rounds using a cutter diameter $1\frac{1}{2}$ inches. Mark out an inner circle, cutting half-way through the pastry, with a cutter diameter $1\frac{1}{4}$ inches or with the point of a knife. Lay these rounds on a lightly buttered baking tin and bake in a 'hot' oven (425F Mark 7) for 15 minutes. When cooked put the cases on a wire rack to cool and remove the inner circles, keep these on one side to use as lids. Hollow out the vol-au-vent cases if necessary and store in an airtight tin until ready to use. *Filling:* melt the butter in a saucepan and add 1 tablespoonful of water and cook the mushrooms for 5 minutes. Remove from the heat and cut the mushrooms in very small pieces. Make the béchamel sauce and add the shrimps, sherry and mushrooms, together with the liquid the latter were cooked in, adjust seasoning. *Mushroom and shrimp vol-au-vent:* spoon the filling into the cases, put a lid on each one, and place in a 'very cool' oven (275F Mark 1) to warm through slowly.

## Sausage Pastry Rings

*Can be prepared 1 day ahead    Action time 30 minutes    Cooking time 15 minutes*

1 lb skinless sausages
$\frac{1}{2}$ lb puff pastry* page 133
1 egg lightly beaten

*Fozen pastry can be used.
The above ingredients make about 40 rings.

Flour a board and roll out the pastry until it is about $\frac{1}{8}$ in. thick. Cut the pastry in strips about 4 in. wide and place the sausages along the strips. Damp one end of the pastry strip and fold it over the sausage to meet the other edge; press the edges firmly together. **At this stage the sausage rings can be kept until the next day.** Brush with egg and bake in a 'hot' oven (425F Mark 7) for 15 minutes. Cut in 1 in. lengths with a sharp knife and serve hot.

## Sausage Balls

*Sausage balls can be prepared and the sauce made 1 day ahead    Action time 20 minutes Cooking time 8 minutes*

$\frac{1}{2}$ lb pork sausage meat
parsley finely chopped
$\frac{1}{2}$ teaspoon prepared mustard
1 egg lightly beaten
flour seasoned with salt and pepper

breadcrumbs
cooking oil for deep fat frying
*Sauce*
$\frac{1}{4}$ pint ($\frac{5}{8}$ cup U.S.) egg mayonnaise, page 127
2 teaspoons Dijon mustard

Mix the sausage meat with the parsley and prepared mustard and divide into 30 small round balls each about ¾ in. in diameter. Dip the balls first in flour, then in egg and lastly in the breadcrumbs; press the latter well in and then shake the balls to get rid of loose crumbs. **At this stage the sausage balls can be put in a covered container and kept in a cool place until the next day.** Heat the oil until a faint haze rises from the pan. Put the balls in a frying basket and immerse them in the oil for 8 minutes. *Sauce:* combine the mustard with the mayonnaise and put it in a small bowl.

Serve the sausage balls hot on cocktail sticks and put the small bowl of sauce in the middle of the plate. The sauce also goes well with hot cocktail sausages.

## Prune and Bacon Rolls

*Action time 10 minutes    Cooking time 20 minutes*

6 rashers streaky bacon
12 large prunes

Pour boiling water on the prunes and leave them to soak for 6 hours. Remove the stones. Trim the rind from the bacon and cut each rasher in half. Wrap the half rashers round the prunes and secure with toothpicks. Cook in a 'moderate' oven (350F Mark 4) for 20 minutes.
Hard cod's roe can also be wrapped in bacon and cooked in the same way.

## Kidney and Bacon Rolls

*Action time 15 minutes    Cooking time 20 minutes*

| | |
|---|---|
| 6 rashers streaky bacon | 1 tablespoon chopped onion |
| 3 lambs kidneys | 1 tablespoon chopped parsley |
| *Stuffing* | pinch of basil |
| 1 small egg lightly beaten | freshly ground pepper |
| 5 tablespoons fresh breadcrumbs | |

Combine the ingredients for the stuffing together in a small bowl. Snip the white membrane from the kidneys and wash them; cut each kidney into four pieces. Trim the rind from the bacon and spread each rasher with the stuffing mixture. Cut each rasher in two and place a piece of kidney on each half. Roll the bacon up and secure with a toothpick. Bake in a  moderate' oven (350F Mark 4) for 20 minutes and serve hot.

## Stuffed Celery

*Action time 20 minutes    No cooking*

6 sticks of celery
1 oz roquefort or Danish blue cheese
1 oz butter
3 ozs cream cheese
½ teaspoon dill
½ teaspoon Worcestershire sauce
paprika for decoration

The above ingredients produce about 30 inch length pieces of stuffed celery.

Put the roquefort or Danish blue, butter, cream cheese, dill and Worcestershire sauce together in a bowl and blend them together using a fork. Scrub and clean the celery sticks thoroughly. Fill the hollow with the cheese mixture and cut into 1 inch lengths; sprinkle with paprika for decoration.

(The chicken liver pâté on page 101 can also be spread on celery sticks.)

# Vegetables

| | | |
|---|---|---|
| Green Salad | *page* | 111 |
| Fennel, Spinach and Avocado Pear Salad | | 111 |
| Apple, Celery and Walnut Salad | | 111 |
| Winter Salad | | 112 |
| Rice Salad | | 112 |
| Tomato Salad | | 112 |
| Tomato Chartreuse | | 113 |
| Ratatouille | | 113 |
| Red Cabbage | | 114 |
| Vegetable Marrow Italian Style | | 114 |
| Braised Celery | | 115 |
| Braised Chicory | | 115 |
| Baked Aubergines with Cheese | | 116 |
| Beetroot with Grapes | | 116 |
| Chou aux Pommes | | 117 |
| Courgettes | | 117 |
| Creamed Spinach | | 117 |
| Baked Carrots | | 118 |
| Potato Crust | | 118 |
| Potato Casserole | | 119 |
| Baked Potatoes | | 119 |
| Boiled Rice | | 120 |
| Spiced Rice | | 120 |
| Rice for Curry | | 121 |
| Rice Pilaff | | 121 |

Green salad, braised and baked vegetables, red cabbage, ratatouille or creamed spinach are the wise selection for the single-handed hostess to choose from. Green vegetables are not on the whole improved either by overcooking or by being kept hot. Young brussels sprouts for instance can take as little as five minutes to cook, and as it is essential to catch them at the right moment, this can present problems if you are trying to entertain guests at the same time. Green vegetables do, however, help to tone down rich food and it is a good move to provide a green salad as well as a hot vegetable if the dish you are serving is a rich one.

Green Salad

Ideally a green salad should be composed of at least three different types of green vegetable, varying in texture and flavour. A combination of cos lettuce, cabbage lettuce and watercress is one green salad. The cos lettuce provides a crisp texture, the cabbage* lettuce a soft one, and the watercress introduces a spicy hot flavour. Other vegetables suitable for this salad are curly endive, spinach, nasturtium leaves and chives.

Wash the salad, pat it gently dry with a tea cloth, taking great care not to bruise it. Put the salad in a plastic bag and store in a refrigerator to crisp the leaves. Dress with sauce vinaigrette, page 128 just before serving, and toss the salad so that each leaf glistens with oil.

*Not all cabbage lettuces have soft leaves, 'Webb's Wonderful' belongs to the crisp variety.

Fennel, Spinach and Avocado Pear Salad

*Action time 10 minutes   No cooking*

1 florence fennel
1 avocado pear
12 small spinach leaves

3 tablespoons sauce vinaigrette, page 128
$\frac{1}{4}$ teaspoon oregano

Wash the fennel and cut any discolouration away from the outside leaf-base; slice into sticks about $\frac{1}{4}$ in. wide. Wash and dry the spinach and tear into mouth-sized pieces. Peel the avocado pear, remove the stone, slice it into about twelve pieces and put it in a bowl. Spoon over the sauce vinaigrette, mix well to ensure that all the avocado pieces have a thin coating of sauce. Add the spinach, fennel and oregano and give a gentle stir. Sliced mozzarella cheese added to this salad makes a delicious first course.

Apple, Celery and Walnut Salad

*Action time about 20 minutes   No cooking*

2 cups (2$\frac{1}{2}$ cups U.S.) $\frac{1}{4}$ in. cubed eating apple
2 cups (2$\frac{1}{2}$ cups U.S.) $\frac{1}{4}$ in. cubed celery
2 ozs walnuts
$\frac{1}{8}$ pint ($\frac{5}{16}$ cup U.S.) sauce vinaigrette, page 128 or egg mayonnaise, page 127

Put all the ingredients together in a salad bowl and pour over the sauce vinaigrette or egg mayonnaise; mix well together.

111

## Winter Salad

*The vegetables can be prepared 1 day ahead    Action time 25 minutes*

4 cups (5 cups U.S.) white cabbage finely sliced
2 cups ($2\frac{1}{2}$ cups U.S.) grated carrot
$\frac{3}{4}$ cup ($1\frac{5}{16}$ cups U.S.) cooked chick peas*
4 cups (5 cups U.S.) cooked beetroot cut in $\frac{1}{4}$ in. cubes
8 tablespoons sultanas
2 tablespoons grated onion (optional)
$\frac{1}{4}$ pint ($\frac{5}{8}$ cup U.S.) sauce vinaigrette, page 128

Makes about 12 cups
*Soak $\frac{1}{4}$ cup of chick peas in water overnight. Place in fresh cold water and bring to the boil; simmer for 45 minutes, strain and cool before using.

Put the cabbage, carrot, beetroot, chick peas, sultanas and onion in a bowl and mix with the sauce vinaigrette.

## Rice Salad

*Can be made 1 day ahead    Action time 20 minutes    No cooking apart from the rice*

$\frac{1}{2}$ lb patna rice
1 tin sweetcorn (about $11\frac{1}{2}$ ozs)
1 tin red pimento (about $4\frac{1}{2}$ ozs)
1 green pepper

4 ozs salted peanuts
$\frac{3}{8}$ pint ($1\frac{5}{16}$ cup U.S.) egg mayonnaise, page 127
1 tablespoon olive oil

Makes about 5 cups.

Cook the rice in fast-boiling water for about 13 minutes. Rinse the rice well under cold running water and drain thoroughly. Place in a bowl and add a tablespoonful of olive oil to keep the grains well separated. Cut the green pepper in half and remove the seeds; dice the flesh into $\frac{1}{4}$ inch cubes. Open the tins of corn and pimento and cut the latter into small pieces. Place the rice, green pepper, sweetcorn, pimento and peanuts in a bowl, pour over the egg mayonnaise and stir with.a fork.

## Tomato Salad

*The tomatoes can be prepared 1 day ahead    Action time 15 minutes    No cooking*

1 lb tomatoes
1 tablespoon finely chopped chives or onion
4 tablespoons sauce vinaigrette, page 128

Baked Potatoes in their jackets

Braised Celery

Summer
Vegetables

Melba Toast

Pour boiling water over the tomatoes to loosen their skins; leave to stand for 1 minute. Peel off the skin and slice the tomatoes in rings. Arrange the slices in a shallow dish, sprinkle over the chives or onion and cover with the sauce vinaigrette.

## Tomato Chartreuse

*Can be made 1 day ahead    Action and cooking time 20 minutes*

| | |
|---|---|
| 1 large tin tomatoes (2 lb 3 ozs) | 2 tablespoons gelatine (enough to set |
| 2 cloves garlic minced or pounded | 2 pints, 5 cups U.S.) |
| 1 tablespoon Worcestershire sauce | 2 bay leaves |
| pinch of thyme | salt and freshly ground pepper |

With the exception of the gelatine, put all the ingredients in a pan and bring them to the boil. Reduce the heat and simmer for 10 minutes. Remove the bay leaves and whisk the tomato with an egg beater to break it up. Take the pan off the stove and allow the mixture to cool for 1 minute before adding the gelatine which has first been left to soak in 6 tablespoons of water. Pour the mixture into a wet angel-food cake tin with a hollow centre and leave to set. Turn the tomato chartreuse out and if you like fill the centre with a mixture of apple, celery and egg mayonnaise or some other kind of salad.

## Ratatouille

*Make 1 day ahead    Action time 30 minutes    Cooking time about 1½ hours*
Serves 4–6

| | |
|---|---|
| 4 courgettes | 4 tablespoons cooking oil |
| 1 aubergine | ⅛ cup ($\frac{5}{16}$ cup U.S.) finely chopped |
| 1 green pepper | parsley |
| 1 onion finely chopped | ⅛ teaspoon salt |
| 1 lb fleshy tomatoes or a 14 oz tin | freshly ground pepper |
| | 2 cloves garlic pounded or minced |

Fry the onion slowly in the oil until it is transparent. Slice the aubergine, courgette and green pepper, first removing the seeds from the latter; add these to the onion together with the garlic, salt and pepper. Cook slowly for ¾ hour stirring occasionally; add the tomatoes and cook for another 30 minutes. Sprinkle in the parsley just before the end of the cooking time.
Ratatouille is equally good eaten hot or cold, and can be served as a first course.

## Red Cabbage

*Make 1 day ahead    Action time 20 minutes    Cooking time 2–2½ hours*
Serves 6–8

2 lbs red cabbage cut finely
⅛ cup (5/16 cup U.S.) vinegar
2 ozs butter
1 tablespoon cooking oil
1 onion finely chopped
1 large cooking apple sliced
½ teaspoon ground cloves

freshly ground pepper
½ teaspoon salt

Melt the butter and oil together in a saucepan and gently fry the onion until it is transparent. Add the red cabbage, vinegar, apple, ground cloves, salt and pepper and cook slowly for at least 2 hours. Stir from time to time to make sure that the cabbage does not stick. Red cabbage improves with keeping so it should preferably be cooked the day before it is needed and reheated.

## Vegetable Marrow Italian Style

*Can be made 1 day ahead    Action time 20 minutes    Cooking time about 35 minutes*
Serves 4

1 vegetable marrow (about 3 lbs weight)
2 tablespoons onion finely chopped
1 tablespoon wine vinegar
2 teaspoons cornflour
1 teaspoon paprika

2 tablespoons cooking oil
¼ teaspoon salt
freshly ground pepper

Peel the skin off the marrow and with a mandolin (universal shredder) cut it into long thin sticks with approximately a ¼ in. diameter. Heat the oil in a pan and gently fry the onion for about 5 minutes. Remove the pan from the fire and stir in the cornflour, then blend in the vinegar, paprika, salt and freshly ground pepper. Add the marrow, return the pan to the fire and simmer over a low heat for about 25–30 minutes stirring from time to time.
It is essential to have a young crisp vegetable marrow for this dish as an older one will tend to disintegrate and become mushy. Reheat in a double boiler or a covered bowl over a pan of simmering water.

**Braised Celery**

*Action time 20 minutes    Cooking time 45 minutes*
Serves 4–6

1 head of celery
$\frac{3}{4}$ pint ($1\frac{7}{8}$ cups U.S.) stock or cube
2 tablespoons flour
1 oz butter
a few drops gravy browning

Wash the celery and scrub the sticks. Remove the outer sticks and keep them on one side to use for soup or stock. Cut each stick in about four pieces. Melt the butter in a saucepan, remove from the heat and blend in the flour to form a roux. Return to the fire and cook until the roux turns very pale straw colour. Draw aside from the fire and stir in the stock a little at a time; add the gravy browning. If you have any gravy left over from a stew or some other meat dish use this in place of some of the stock. Butter a shallow fireproof dish and cook in a 'moderate' oven (350F Mark 4) for 45 minutes.

**Braised Chicory**

*Action time 10 minutes    Cooking time 1 hour*
Serves 4

$1\frac{1}{2}$ lbs chicory
juice of half a lemon
1 tablespoon olive oil
1 oz butter
salt and freshly ground pepper

Wash the chicory and remove any brown parts from the leaves. Cook for 5 minutes in salted simmering water. Remove the chicory from the pan and drain for 2 to 3 minutes. Next place the chicory in an ovenproof dish together with the butter, oil, lemon juice, salt and pepper. Put a lid on the dish and bake in a 'moderate' oven (350F Mark 4) for about 1 hour. Braised chicory can be reheated.

## Baked Aubergines with Cheese

*Can be prepared 1 day ahead*    *Action time 15 minutes*    *Cooking time 55 minutes*
Serves 6

3 aubergines
3 rounded tablespoons grated cheese
1 oz butter
dried breadcrumbs
freshly ground pepper
salt

Parboil the aubergines for 25 minutes and remove them from the pan. Split them in half lengthways and gently scrape out the pulp. Put the pulp in a bowl with the cheese, salt and pepper and mix well together. Spoon the pulp mixture into the aubergine shells, cover with breadcrumbs and dot with butter. **At this point the aubergines can be kept until the next day.** Bake in a 'moderate' oven (350F Mark 4) for 30 minutes.
Baked aubergines with cheese also make a delicious first course.

## Beetroot with Grapes

*Can be partly cooked 1 day ahead and the grapes prepared*    *Action time 25 minutes*
*Cooking time 2 hours*
Serves 6

1½ lbs beetroot
6 ozs grapes
¾ pint (1⅞ cups U.S.) white sauce, page 123
salt

Wash the beetroot taking great care not to break the skin; do not cut off the roots and only trim the stalks. Place in a saucepan and cover with salted boiling water; simmer for 1½ hours. Remove the pan from the fire, and drain and skin the beetroot. Peel and de-seed the grapes. **At this point the beetroot and grapes can be kept until the next day.** Make the white sauce. Slice the beetroot and arrange it in a casserole dish, sprinkle over the grapes and pour on the sauce. Put a lid on the casserole and bake in a 'moderate' oven (350F Mark 4) for 30 minutes.

## Chou aux Pommes

*Action time 20 minutes   Cooking time 1 hour*
Serves 6

1½ lbs white cabbage
1 lb cooking apples
3 tablespoons vinegar
¼ teaspoon nutmeg

1 oz butter
salt and pepper

Shred the cabbage and peel, core and slice the apples. Place in alternate layers in a casserole, pour over the vinegar, cover with nutmeg, add salt and pepper and dot with knobs of butter. Bake in a 'moderate' oven (350F Mark 4) for about 1 hour.

## Baked Courgettes

*Action time 10 minutes   Cooking time 35 minutes*
Serves 4

1½ lbs courgettes
1 oz butter
2 tablespoons olive oil
1 tablespoon lemon juice

finely chopped parsley
salt and pepper

Slice each courgette into about 6 rings and place on a sheet of tin foil. Pour over the oil and lemon juice, dot with butter. Season well with salt and pepper and wrap in foil. Bake in a 'moderate' oven (350F Mark 4) for about 35 minutes. Sprinkle with parsley before serving.

## Creamed Spinach

*Can be made 1 day ahead and reheated   Action time 40 minutes*
*Cooking time 25 minutes*
Serves 6

4 lbs spinach
¼ pint (⅝ cup U.S.) double cream
1 oz butter
1 tablespoon flour

1 tablespoon lemon juice
salt
freshly ground pepper

Remove the stalks from the spinach and wash it thoroughly, changing the water several times during the process. Put it into a large pan or 2 pans if necessary with salt and cook over a low flame for about 20 minutes; the water clinging to the leaves after washing provides sufficient moisture. Strain well in a sieve, pressing down firmly to remove all liquid, and put through a Mouli. **At this stage the spinach can be kept until the next day.** Melt the butter in a saucepan, blend in the flour and cook for 1 to 2 minutes before adding the spinach, lemon juice, pepper and additional salt, if necessary. Warm the spinach through and add the cream just before serving.

## Baked Carrots

*Action time 10 minutes    Cooking time 45 minutes*
Serves 6

    1 lb small carrots
    2 tablespoons demerara sugar
    1½ ozs butter
    1 tablespoon lemon juice
    salt and pepper
    finely chopped parsley

Sit the carrots on a sheet of tinfoil and cover with knobs of butter, sugar and lemon juice; add salt and pepper. Wrap the foil over and bake in a 'moderate' oven (350F Mark 4) for 45 minutes or until the carrots are tender. Serve sprinkled with finely chopped parsley.

## Potato Crust

*Action time 20 minutes    Cooking time about 30 minutes*

    1½ lbs potatoes
    3 tablespoons milk
    1 egg lightly beaten
    1 oz butter
    salt and pepper
    The above produces 2 cups (2½ cups U.S.) of mashed potato.

Peel the potatoes and boil them in salted water for 25–30 minutes until they are tender. Strain the potatoes and add the egg, butter, milk, salt and pepper. Mash and whip them with a fork until they are smooth and creamy. Keep in a warm place until ready to use.

118

## Potato Casserole

*The potatoes and cheese can be prepared 1 day ahead    Action time 30 minutes*
*Cooking time 50 minutes*
Serves 4

| | |
|---|---|
| 1 lb potatoes | 2 ozs butter |
| 1 egg lightly beaten | salt and pepper |
| ½ pint (1¼ cups U.S.) milk | 1 clove garlic minced or pounded |
| 1½ tablespoons flour | (optional) |
| ¼ lb grated cheddar cheese | |

Peel the potatoes and cut them in thin slices. Make a white sauce with the flour, milk and half the butter; add the garlic, salt and pepper. Take the pan off the stove, add the cheese and then the egg stirring as you do so. Place a layer of potatoes in the bottom of a casserole and pour on some of the sauce. Repeat this process until all the potatoes have been used and finish with a layer of sauce; scatter knobs of butter over the surface and bake in a 'moderate' oven (350F Mark 4) for 50 minutes. If you prepare the potatoes the day before cooking them, keep in cold water and dry them throughly with a tea cloth before using. The grated cheese should be kept in a cool place in a covered container.


## Baked Potatoes

*Cooking time about 1½ hours*

Scrub the potatoes thoroughly before baking and prick their skins in two or three places with a skewer. It is difficult to give exact timing for baking potatoes as this depends to a large extent on their type and size. A medium to large potato will take about 1½ hours to cook in a 'warm to moderate' oven (325–350F Mark 3–4). Serve split open and fill either with a mixture of soured cream and chives or with plenty of butter


## Rice

Rice is suggested as an accompaniment to many dishes in this book, and it may be useful to remember that 2 ozs per person is a reasonable amount to allow, and also that rice more or less trebles its bulk once it is cooked. As rice absorbs varying amounts of liquid according to the moisture in its makeup, it is impossible to be exact about the amounts of liquid needed for cooking methods which rely on the absorption of all liquid. This difficulty can, however, be overcome either by adding more stock or water during the cooking or by cooking the rice for a few minutes longer if there is slightly too much liquid. Rice should be well washed before cooking in order to remove loose surface starch. Stand it in a bowl of water for about 15 minutes and change the water several times until it remains reasonably clear. You will find that rice bought loose needs more washing than the packaged variety.

## Boiled Rice

*Action time 10 minutes    Cooking time about 10 minutes*
Serves 4–6

¾ lb patna rice
5 pints water (12½ cups U.S.)
lemon juice (optional)
salt

Wash the rice. Bring the water to the boil and when it is fast-boiling add the rice in a steady stream together with the salt and lemon juice; the latter ensures that the rice remains white. At the end of the cooking time the rice should be firm, and it is wise to start testing after about 10 minutes as overcooked rice quickly becomes mushy and spoilt. Drain the rice in a colander and run cold or hot water through it to remove any remaining starch. To dry the rice either place it in a flat dish and put it in a cool oven, in which case turn it with a fork from time to time, or melt a little butter in a saucepan and place the rice in this; stand in a warm corner on top of the stove, cover with a cloth and shake the pan from time to time.

## Spiced Rice

*Action time 10 minutes    Cooking time 40 minutes*
Serves 4–6

¾ lb patna or Italian rice
1¼ pints (3⅛ cups U.S.) beef stock or cube
4 tablespoons cooking oil

½ teaspoon ground cumin
¼ teaspoon ground cloves
salt

Wash the rice and dry with a cloth. Put the oil in a saucepan and when a faint haze rises from the pan add the rice. Fry it for about 5 minutes stirring from time to time and add the ground cumin, cloves and salt. Remove the pan from the stove and slowly add the stock. Return to the fire and bring to the boil. Place the contents of the pan in a casserole without a lid and put in a 'moderate' oven (350F Mark 4) for about 35 minutes until all the liquid has been absorbed.

**Rice for Curry**

*Action time 10 minutes   Cooking time about 20 minutes*
Serves 4

$\frac{1}{2}$ lb patna or Italian rice
1$\frac{1}{2}$ ozs butter
generous $\frac{1}{2}$ pint (1$\frac{1}{4}$ cups U.S.) water
4 inch-size pieces of cinnamon
6 cardamoms
salt

Wash the rice and place it in a saucepan together with the water, salt, cardamoms and cinnamon; put the butter on the top and put a lid on the pan. Bring to the boil over a low flame and continue cooking for about 15–20 minutes, do not stir the rice but check from time to time to make sure there is enough liquid. Remove the cardamoms and cinnamon before serving.

**Rice Pilaff**

*Action time 15 minutes   Cooking time about 25 minutes*

$\frac{1}{2}$ lb patna or Italian rice
1 pint (2$\frac{1}{2}$ cups U.S.) chicken stock or cube
1 small onion finely sliced
$\frac{1}{4}$ lb mushrooms thinly sliced
2 ozs butter
1 teaspoon oregano
salt

Wash the rice. Melt half the butter in a pan and fry the onion until it is transparent, add the rice and oregano and cook for 1–2 minutes. Pour on the stock, add the salt and put a lid on the pan. Bring to simmering point and cook slowly for 15–20 minutes until all the stock has been absorbed; add more liquid if necessary. Just before the end of the cooking time melt the remaining butter in a pan, gently sauté the mushrooms and add them to the rice.

# Sauces

| | | |
|---|---|---|
| White Sauce | *page* | 123 |
| Béchamel Sauce | | 123 |
| Sauce Espagnole | | 124 |
| Brown Sauce | | 124 |
| Simple Gravy | | 125 |
| Tomato Sauce I | | 125 |
| Tomato Sauce II | | 126 |
| White Wine Sauce | | 126 |
| Bread Sauce | | 126 |
| Egg Mayonnaise | | 127 |
| Blender Mayonnaise | | 127 |
| Blender Hollandaise | | 128 |
| Sauce Vinaigrette | | 128 |
| Aïoli Sauce | | 129 |
| Custard Sauce | | 129 |
| Chocolate Sauce I | | 129 |
| Chocolate Sauce II | | 130 |
| Chocolate Cream | | 130 |
| Brandy Butter | | 131 |

## White Sauce (1 pint)

*Action and cooking time 15 minutes*

1 pint (2½ cups U.S.) milk
3 tablespoons flour
1 oz butter
pepper and salt

Put the milk in a pan and bring to scalding point. In another pan gently melt the butter. Draw the pan aside from the stove and blend the flour with the butter and add the salt and pepper. Return the pan to the heat, and cook the roux until it begins to bubble and turn a very pale straw colour. Remove the roux from the fire, and slowly stir in the scalded milk, return to the heat and bring to the boil. Cook for 2 to 3 minutes, stirring all the time.

The above is a pouring sauce; to make a coating sauce add 1½ additional tablespoonfuls of flour and ½ oz of butter.

## Béchamel Sauce (1 pint)

*Action and cooking time 15 minutes*

1 pint (2½ cups U.S.) milk
3 tablespoons flour
1 oz butter
bouquet garni
half an onion
peppercorns
salt

Put the milk in a saucepan and add the onion, bouquet garni, peppercorns and salt and bring slowly to scalding temperature over a very low flame; do not allow to boil. Remove the bouquet garni, onion and peppercorns. In another saucepan melt the butter; set the saucepan aside from the flame and blend in the flour to form a roux. Return the pan to the fire and cook the roux until it bubbles and begins to slightly turn colour. Remove the roux from the heat and slowly blend in the scalded milk, return to the fire and bring to boiling point. Cook for a further 2 to 3 minutes stirring all the time.

The above is a pouring sauce but if you want a coating sauce add 1½ additional tablespoonfuls of flour and a ½ oz of butter.

## Sauce Espagnole

*Can be made 1 day ahead    Action time 30 minutes    Cooking time 2–3 hours*

1½ cups (1⅞ cups U.S.) onion finely
    chopped
1 cup (1¼ cups U.S.) grated carrot
½ cup (⅝ cup U.S.) finely chopped celery
1 tablespoon bacon diced
1 teaspoon tomato paste
gravy browning*

¼ pint (⅝ cup U.S.) red wine (optional)
2½ pints (6¼ cups U.S.) beef stock or
    cube
3 rounded tablespoons flour
8 peppercorns
2–3 ozs butter
salt

Makes 2 cups.
*See use of caramel in the recipe below.

Melt the butter in a saucepan and slowly sauté the onion, carrot, celery and bacon
for about 5 minutes. Add the flour and, stirring all the time, cook for a few minutes.
Meanwhile in another saucepan heat the stock to scalding temperature. Take the
pan with the vegetables off the fire and add the warmed stock, stirring and blending
it carefully with the flour and vegetables as you do so. Return to the fire, add the
tomato paste, red wine, caramel or gravy browning, peppercorns and salt. Simmer
for 2 to 3 hours until the stock is reduced by more than half. Sieve before serving.

## Brown Sauce

*Can be made 1 day ahead    Action time 15 minutes    Cooking time 20 minutes*

1 carrot grated
1 small onion finely chopped
1 oz butter
¾ pint (1⅞ cups U.S.) beef stock
    or cube
2 tablespoons sherry (optional)
2 teaspoons flour

¼ teaspoon French mustard
⅛ teaspoon salt
freshly ground pepper
1 bay leaf
1 tablespoon sugar for caramel or a few
    drops of gravy browning

Melt the butter in a saucepan and gently fry the onion and carrot for 5 minutes. Add
the flour and continue cooking for a further 2 minutes before placing the stock, bay
leaf, mustard, salt and pepper in the saucepan. Meanwhile, in another saucepan put
1 tablespoon of water with the sugar and, stirring, boil until the syrup turns dark
brown (alternatively use gravy browning though you will loose the bitter taste the

caramel provides); add to the stock in the pan. Simmer for 20 minutes stirring occasionally. Remove from the fire, put half the vegetables through a sieve and discard the remainder. Return the liquid and the sieved vegetables to the pan and add the sherry, reheat and serve.

### Simple Gravy (For Meat and Game)

*Can be prepared 1 day ahead   Action time 5 minutes   Cooking time 5 minutes*

$\frac{1}{2}$ pint (1$\frac{1}{4}$ cups U.S.) stock or cube
   or stock and wine half-and-half
1 slightly rounded tablespoon flour
gravy browning*
salt and pepper
$\frac{1}{4}$ pint ($\frac{5}{8}$ cup U.S.) soured cream (optional)

*See use of caramel in the recipe for Brown Sauce.

Put the flour in a cup and blend in the stock a little at a time. Add the salt, pepper and caramel or gravy browning. After you have removed the meat or game to a carving dish, tip all but 2 tablespoonfuls of fat out of the roasting pan. Return the pan to the fire and pour on the gravy mixture stirring as you do so. Bring to the boil, turn down the heat and simmer for 2 or 3 minutes. Soured cream can be added to the gravy just before serving; take care not to boil.

### Tomato Sauce I

*Can be made 1 day ahead   Action time 10 minutes   Cooking time 35 minutes*

| | |
|---|---|
| 1 lb fleshy tomatoes sliced | 4 tablespoons beurre manié, page 133 |
| $\frac{1}{4}$ pint ($\frac{5}{8}$ cup U.S.) red wine | 1 teaspoon basil |
| $\frac{1}{4}$ pint ($\frac{5}{8}$ cup U.S.) beef stock or cube | salt |
| $\frac{1}{2}$ medium-sized onion finely chopped | freshly ground pepper |
| 2 tablespoons olive oil | 1 clove garlic minced or pounded (optional) |

Makes 1 pint (2$\frac{1}{2}$ cups U.S.) – half the above ingredients again will be needed to make enough sauce to go with the meat loaf for 10 on page 70.

Heat the oil in a saucepan and gently sauté the onion for 2 or 3 minutes before adding the sliced tomato, basil, garlic, salt and pepper; cook for a further 10 minutes. Blend in the beurre manié and then add the red wine and stock. Simmer for 20 minutes and sieve before serving.

## Tomato Sauce II

*Can be made 1 day ahead    Action time 10 minutes    Cooking time 30 minutes*

| | |
|---|---|
| 1 tin tomatoes (about 14 ozs) | 2 tablespoons sherry |
| $\frac{1}{2}$ pint (1$\frac{1}{4}$ cups U.S.) beef stock or cube | 1 teaspoon Worcestershire sauce |
| $\frac{1}{2}$ medium-sized onion finely chopped | 2 bay leaves |
| 1 oz butter | salt |
| 2 tablespoons flour | freshly ground pepper |

Makes generous $\frac{3}{4}$ pint (2 cups U.S.)

Melt the butter in a saucepan and gently fry the onion for a few minutes. Add the flour and stir to a roux with the onion, cook for 1 to 2 minutes before blending in the tomatoes and stock. Add the Worcestershire sauce, sherry, bay leaves, salt and pepper and simmer for 25 minutes. Sieve before serving.

## White Wine Sauce

*Can be made 1 day ahead    Action time 10 minutes    Cooking time about 35 minutes*

| | |
|---|---|
| $\frac{1}{3}$ pint ($\frac{7}{8}$ cup U.S.) fish stock* | 1 oz butter |
| $\frac{1}{3}$ pint ($\frac{7}{8}$ cup U.S.) milk | pinch of mace |
| $\frac{1}{3}$ pint ($\frac{7}{8}$ cup U.S.) white wine | $\frac{1}{4}$ teaspoon fennel seeds |
| $\frac{1}{2}$ small onion finely chopped | 8 peppercorns |
| 2 tablespoons flour | salt |

*See culinary terms, page 140.

Melt the butter in a pan and gently fry the onion. Add the flour and stirring all the time cook for 2 or 3 minutes. Remove from the fire and add a little of the fish stock, blending it carefully into the flour and onion. Return the pan to the fire, add the rest of the fish stock and the milk, mace, peppercorns, fennel and salt and bring to the boil stirring as you do so. Add the wine and continue cooking, stirring occasionally, until the sauce has reduced by half, this will take about 30 minutes. Strain and the sauce is then ready to serve.

## Bread Sauce

*Breadcrumbs can be prepared 1 day ahead    Action time 20 minutes*
*Cooking time 30 minutes*
Serves 4–6

| | |
|---|---|
| 1 cup (1$\frac{1}{4}$ cups U.S.) fresh white breadcrumbs | 1 pint (2$\frac{1}{2}$ cups U.S.) milk |
| 1 onion studded with cloves | salt and freshly ground pepper |

Place the milk and onion in a saucepan and bring slowly to scalding temperature. Add salt and pepper. Move the saucepan from the heat and leave to stand for 30 minutes or longer. Return the pan to the heat, add the breadcrumbs and cook slowly for 20 minutes stirring from time to time to prevent the bread from sticking to the bottom of the pan. Remove the onion and cloves. Keep the sauce hot in a double boiler.

The quantities given above produce generous helpings for 4; double this amount would be adequate for 12 with turkey.

## Egg Mayonnaise

*Can be made 1 day ahead   Action time 20 minutes*

| | |
|---|---|
| 2 egg yolks | $\frac{1}{4}$ teaspoon salt |
| $\frac{1}{2}$ pint (1$\frac{1}{4}$ cups U.S.) olive oil | a little dry mustard (optional) |
| 2–3 teaspoons lemon juice or wine or tarragon vinegar, or a mixture | white pepper |

Put the egg yolks in a small mixing bowl. If you haven't got a cork with a dropper for the oil, place some of the oil in a small jug with a good pouring lip. Add one teaspoon of lemon juice or vinegar to the egg yolks; add the salt, pepper and dry mustard and blend these ingredients well together for 1 minute using a wooden spoon. Then stirring briskly all the time add the oil drop by drop with the other hand. After about 10 minutes the mixture should start to thicken. Once the sauce starts to thicken the oil can be poured on in a thin steady stream. Add the rest of the vinegar, taste and season further if necessary. This sauce can be eaten at once or stored in an airtight container in a cool place but not a refrigerator. If the oil and egg separates during the preparation of the mayonnaise, start the process all over again using 1 egg yolk and 1 teaspoon of lemon juice or vinegar. These ingredients should be well blended together before adding 1 tablespoon of oil drop by drop; then very slowly pour on the separated mayonnaise stirring all the time with the other hand.

## Blender Mayonnaise

*Can be made 1 day ahead   Action time 10 minutes*

| | |
|---|---|
| 1 whole egg | 1 teaspoon sugar |
| $\frac{1}{2}$ pint (1$\frac{1}{4}$ cups U.S.) olive oil | $\frac{1}{2}$ teaspoon salt |
| 2–3 teaspoons lemon juice or wine vinegar | a little dry mustard (optional) |

Put the egg, lemon juice or vinegar, salt, sugar and mustard in to a blender. Cover and blend until the ingredients are well combined. With the motor still running, very slowly pour the olive oil on to the egg mixture. Continue to blend until the mayonnaise has thickened. If the sauce separates and fails to thicken carry out the same rescue operation as for mayonnaise made by hand.

### Blender Hollandaise Sauce

*Action and cooking time 10 minutes*

3 egg yolks
2 tablespoons lemon juice
8 ozs butter
$\frac{1}{4}$ teaspoon salt
white pepper

Put the yolks in the blender together with the lemon juice, salt and pepper and blend at high for 2 or 3 seconds only. Meanwhile melt the butter in a saucepan until it bubbles. Remove the centre lid in the top of the blender or raise the whole lid slightly to one side, switch the motor to high and pour in the bubbling butter. By the time you have finished pouring the butter the sauce should be made.

### Sauce Vinaigrette

*Can be made 1 day ahead   Action time 10 minutes   No cooking*

$\frac{1}{8}$ pint ($\frac{5}{16}$ cup U.S.) wine vinegar or lemon
  juice and vinegar half-and-half
$\frac{3}{8}$ pint ($1\frac{5}{16}$ cup U.S.) olive oil
$\frac{1}{4}$ teaspoon salt
$\frac{1}{4}$ teaspoon dry mustard
freshly ground pepper
1 clove garlic minced or pounded (optional)

Beat the vinegar or lemon juice, pepper, salt, mustard and garlic together with a wooden spoon. Slowly pour on the oil and blend well. A little castor sugar or Dijon mustard can also be added to this dressing.

*above* STAGES IN MAKING
SHORT CRUST PASTRY

*above left* rubbing in the fat
*above right* gathering the dough
into shape

*left* blending ingredients for
Profiteroles

*below* LINING A FLAN RING

*left* tucking pastry into flan case
*centre* filling flan case with beans
*right* lifting the flan case off the
baked pastry shell

## Aïoli Sauce

*Can be made 1 day ahead    Action time 20 minutes    No cooking*

4 cloves garlic minced or pounded
2 egg yolks
1 cup (1¼ cups U.S.) olive oil
2 teaspoons lemon juice
¼ teaspoon salt

Put the egg yolks, garlic, 1 teaspoonful of lemon juice and the salt together in a bowl. Stir with a wooden spoon until the ingredients are well combined. Add the olive oil drop by drop as for egg mayonnaise until the sauce thickens. Once the sauce has thickened add the second teaspoonful of lemon juice and the remaining oil which can now be poured in a thin steady stream. Should the ailloli sauce fail to thicken start again as you would for failed egg mayonnaise.

This delicious sauce is for garlic lovers only, it is good eaten with cold fish but can also be served with sticks of carrot, celery and cauliflower as a first course.

## Custard Sauce

*Can be made 1 day ahead    Action and cooking time 10 minutes*

1 large egg                          ½ tablespoon castor sugar
½ pint (1¼ cups U.S.) milk           few drops vanilla essence

Put the milk in a saucepan and bring it slowly to scalding temperature. Meanwhile beat the egg in a basin with the sugar. Pour the milk onto the egg stirring all the time. Add the vanilla essence and return the mixture to the saucepan. Cook over a low flame stirring all the time and taking care that the custard does not boil. The custard is ready to serve as soon as it thickens. If using to pour over a summer pudding allow it to cool first.

## Chocolate Sauce I

*Can be made 1 day ahead    Action and cooking time 45 minutes*

4 ozs plain chocolate broken in small pieces
4 ozs butter
8 ozs castor sugar
½ pint (1¼ cups U.S.) milk
1 teaspoon rum or a few drops of vanilla

Melt the butter and chocolate together, do not boil. Add the sugar and milk and stir over a low heat until the sugar completely dissolves. Boil for 35–45 minutes. Remove from the heat and add the rum or vanilla drops. The sauce is now ready to serve, but it can if necessary be kept hot, or be reheated, in a double boiler or in a bowl over a pan of simmering water. It will tend to crystallize if kept hot for more than about 1 hour.

## Chocolate Sauce II

*Can be made 1 day ahead    Action and cooking time 10 minutes*

4 ozs plain chocolate broken in small pieces
$\frac{1}{4}$ pint ($\frac{5}{8}$ cup U.S.) milk
4 tablespoons icing sugar
$\frac{1}{2}$ oz butter

Put the ingredients together in a pan and slowly bring to boiling point. Boil for 5 minutes and remove from the fire. Either serve hot with ice-cream or cold with profiteroles.
To give a slight orange flavour add the grated peel of an orange and one tablespoonful of juice.

## Chocolate Cream

*Can be made 1 day ahead    Action and cooking time 25 minutes*

4 ozs chocolate broken in small pieces
1 egg yolk
$\frac{1}{8}$ pint ($\frac{5}{16}$ cup U.S.) single cream or
    milk
3 tablespoons castor sugar

$\frac{1}{2}$ tablespoon cornflour
$\frac{1}{2}$ oz butter
1 drop vanilla
$\frac{1}{4}$ pint ($\frac{5}{8}$ cup U.S.) double cream

Blend the egg yolk, cornflour and sugar together in the top of a double boiler or in a basin over simmering water; add the single cream, butter and chocolate and also the vanilla. Cook until the mixture thickens, stirring from time to time during this process – it will take about 20 minutes. Remove from the heat and allow to get cold. Whisk the double cream until it is stiff and fold it into the chocolate mixture. Use to fill profiteroles.

**Brandy Butter**

*Can be made 1 day ahead   Action time 10 minutes   No cooking*

$\frac{1}{2}$ lb butter
6 ozs icing sugar
6 tablespoons brandy or 3 tablespoons rum

Cream the butter and sugar together and slowly work in the brandy or rum.

# Miscellaneous

Beurre Manié *page* 133
Short crust Pastry 133
Puff Pastry 133
Garlic Bread 134
Melba Toast 134
Croûtons 135
Fried Breadcrumbs 135
Macaroons 135
Poppadums 136
Batter 136
Forcemeat 136
Chestnut Stuffing 137
Boiled Chicken 137
Poached Eggs 138

**Beurre Manié** (for thickening stock)

*Can be made ahead and stored   Action time 10 minutes*

8 tablespoons flour
¼ lb butter

Cream the butter and flour together with a fork until completely blended. Store in a covered container in a cool place or a refrigerator and use as required. This is the most satisfactory way of adding flour to stock to thicken it. Stir 1–2 tablespoonfuls of beurre manié at a time into the stock and stir carefully; simmer for a few minutes before serving.

If you do not have time to prepare beurre manié, blend the flour 1–2 tablespoons at a time, with an equal part of water, and then add a little of the hot stock to this mixture stirring carefully as you do so. Add this well blended mixture to the stock you want to thicken; stir and then simmer for 2 to 3 minutes before serving.

**Short Crust Pastry**

*Can be made 1 day ahead   Action time 15 minutes*

| | |
|---|---|
| 6 ozs plain flour | 1½ ozs lard |
| 1½ ozs butter | ¼ teaspoon salt |

Sift the flour and salt into a basin. Cut the fat in small pieces and add this to the flour. Mix either by lightly running the flour and fat between your finger tips and your thumb or by using a pastry mixer, until the mixture looks like fine breadcrumbs. Mix to a stiff dough with water. **At this point the dough can be wrapped in tinfoil and kept in a cool place or refrigerator until the next day.** Turn on to a floured board, knead into a neat shape and then roll to the required thickness. Try to keep the shape you want to achieve as you roll, pastry does not improve by being rolled twice.

**Puff Pastry**

*Action time 30 minutes   Cooking and standing time about 2 hours*

| | |
|---|---|
| 6 ozs plain flour | ice-cold water for mixing |
| 6 ozs butter well chilled | ½ teaspoon salt |
| juice of 1 lemon chilled | |

Sieve the flour and salt and mix to a soft dough with the juice of a lemon and a little cold water. Put the dough on a well floured board and knead it lightly for a minute or two; roll into a long rectangle and leave to stand for 25 minutes in a very cool place. Place the butter between two pieces of grease proof paper and flatten it so that it will cover $\frac{1}{3}$ of the rectangle. Place the butter in the centre of the rectangle of dough and fold the ends over to cover it. Roll again to a long rectangle and fold in three, cover with greaseproof paper and leave to stand in a cool place for 12 minutes. Repeat the rolling, folding and waiting process 6 times. Roll from the open and not the folded edge to ensure that the dough is rolled in a different direction each time. **At the end of the rolling the pastry can be kept in the refrigerator until the next day.** Roll the pastry into the shape and thickness required and leave to stand for a further 30 minutes. Cook in a 'hot' oven (425F Mark 7) for 20–30 minutes depending on the dish being made.

## Garlic Bread

*Action time 10 minutes    Cooking time 20 minutes*

1 medium-sized French loaf
3 cloves garlic minced or pounded
$\frac{1}{4}$ lb butter

Melt the butter in a saucepan and add the garlic. Slice the French bread, taking care not to cut all the way through so that the slices are held together by the bottom crust. Stand the French loaf on a piece of tinfoil. Separate the slices of bread slightly and pour a little melted butter on to each. Wrap the tinfoil over the bread and bake in a 'fairly hot' oven (375F Mark 5) for 20 minutes.

## Melba Toast

*Can be made 1 day ahead    Cooking time 45 minutes*

Cut the bread in very thin slices and remove the crusts. Bake until crisp and light brown in a 'very cool' oven (275F Mark 1) for about 45 minutes. Cool and keep in an airtight tin.

**Croûtons**

*Action and cooking time 12 minutes*
Serves 4

    1 cup (1¼ cups U.S.) stale* bread cut in ¼ in. ·cubes
    about 1½ ozs butter

*If stale bread is not available use fresh bread but toast it first before cutting into cubes.

Melt the butter in a frying pan and when it starts to bubble add the bread cubes. Sauté them gently for about 10 minutes and turn from time to time so that the bread browns on all sides. If too much butter has been used in the cooking the croûtons will appear greasy, in which case they should be drained on a piece of absorbent paper.

**Fried Breadcrumbs**

*Action and cooking time 5 minutes*

    12 tablespoons dried breadcrumbs
    2 ozs butter

Melt the butter in a pan and when it is hot and foaming add the breadcrumbs. Shake the pan from time to time to prevent the breadcrumbs from sticking. They will take about 3 to 4 minutes to brown.
Try to avoid using golden breadcrumbs sold in packets, either make your own by drying bread slowly in the oven and crushing it with a rolling pin or buy dried breadcrumbs from a bakery.

**Macaroons**

*Action time 10 minutes   Cooking time 15 minutes*

    1 large egg white            split almonds (decoration)
    2½ ozs ground almonds      rice paper
    4 ozs castor sugar          1 egg white for glazing
    1–2 teaspoons water

The above ingredients produce about 24 small macaroons, or 8 large macaroons suitable for eating at tea-time.

Whisk the egg white until stiff. Mix the ground almonds, sugar and water together and fold in the white of egg. Cover a buttered baking sheet with rice paper and using a small teaspoon put mounds of the mixture on the rice paper. Place half a split almond on each one, brush with a little white of egg and bake in a 'moderate' oven (350F Mark 4) for about 15 minutes

## Poppadums

*Cooking time 30 seconds each*

These are eaten with curry and can be bought in most supermarkets. Heat sufficient cooking oil in a frying pan to cover a poppadum. As soon as a faint haze rises from the fat cook the poppadums one at a time; they only take about 30 seconds to cook. Remove from the pan with a fish slice and place on absorbent paper to drain off any excess oil. They can be kept hot for several hours in a low oven.

## Batter

*Action time 10 minutes*

$\frac{1}{4}$ lb flour
$\frac{1}{2}$ pint (1$\frac{1}{4}$ cups U.S.) milk
1 egg
pinch of salt

Sieve the flour and salt together in to a bowl; make a slight hollow in the centre and drop in the egg and $\frac{1}{3}$ of the milk. Gradually combine the flour, egg and milk to make a smooth paste without any lumps. Beat well with a wooden spoon and slowly add the rest of the milk. Cover and stand for at least 30 minutes in a cool place.

## Forcemeat

*Can be prepared 1 day ahead   Action time 20 minutes*

| | |
|---|---|
| 1$\frac{1}{2}$ cups (1$\frac{7}{8}$ cups U.S.) fresh bread-crumbs | $\frac{1}{2}$ teaspoon thyme |
| | the rind and juice of 1 lemon |
| 3 ozs suet | salt and pepper |
| 2 eggs lightly beaten | 1$\frac{1}{2}$ ozs butter – for forcemeat rissoles |
| 4 tablespoons chopped parsley | |

Prepare half as much again when stuffing turkey for twelve.

Mix all the ingredients together and season with the salt and pepper. This mixture can either be used to stuff a turkey or rolled into small rissoles and eaten with jugged hare. Fry the rissoles in butter until they are brown on each side and add to the hare in the casserole.

### Chestnut Stuffing

*Can be prepared 1 day ahead    Action time 35 minutes    Cooking time 45 minutes*

1½ lbs chestnuts
1½ cups (1⅞ cups U.S.) fresh breadcrumbs
2 eggs lightly beaten
2 ozs butter
salt and pepper

Slit the chestnuts and boil them in salted water for 45 minutes until they are tender. Shell the chestnuts and put them in a bowl. Add the eggs, breadcrumbs, butter, salt and pepper and mix these ingredients well together. The stuffing is now ready for use.

### Boiled Chicken

*Can be cooked 1 day ahead    Action time 1½ hours    Cooking time 1½–2 hours*

1 boiling fowl* weight about 4½–5 lbs    8 peppercorns
when dressed (approximately 4–5 cups    2 bouquet garni
(5–6 cups U.S.) cooked chicken)    1 stick celery (optional)
1 onion    salt
1 carrot
2 bay leaves

*If using a smaller chicken the cooking time should be reduced.

Place the chicken together with the other ingredients in a large saucepan or flame-proof casserole. Add enough water to almost cover the chicken, put a lid on the pan and slowly simmer for 1½–2 hours until the bird is tender and the skin comes away easily. Remove the pan from the fire and take out the chicken. The skin and flesh should be removed as soon as it is possible to do so without burning your fingers; discard the skin. If the flesh is to be eaten in a cream sauce take a pair of scissors and cut the chicken into thin slices measuring about 2 inches long. For chicken vol-au-vent cut the flesh into small cubes. For a good chicken stock, return the pan to the stove, add the carcass and boil for 30 minutes or longer until the liquid has considerably reduced. Leave to cool and skim off the surplus fat before using.

## Poached Eggs

*Can be prepared 1 day ahead   Action time about 10 minutes*
*Cooking time about 5 minutes*

4 eggs
1 teaspoon vinegar
$\frac{1}{8}$ teaspoon salt

There are several methods for poaching eggs, one easy way is to use a frying pan and circular pastry cutters. Place the pastry cutters in the frying pan together with enough water to cover the eggs; add the vinegar and salt and bring to the boil. Meanwhile break the first egg into a small cup. Lower the heat and slide the egg into a pastry cutter; swiftly repeat the process for the other three eggs and leave over a low heat for about 5 minutes until the whites of egg are firm. Gently remove from the pan with the aid of a fish slice and drain well. Place in a pan of cold water if the eggs are to be kept until the next day. They will quickly warm through if served on a well heated plate with a hot sauce.

# Measurements

1 English Cup = 10 fluid ounces = $\frac{1}{2}$ English pint
1 American cup = 8 fluid ounces = $\frac{1}{2}$ American pint

| British | American Approximate Equivalent | Metric Approximate Equivalent |
|---|---|---|
| 3 ozs breadcrumbs – fresh | $1\frac{3}{4}$ cups | 85 grams |
| 8 ozs butter or other fat | 1 cup | 227 grams |
| 1 oz butter | 2 tablespoons | 28 grams |
| 4 ozs cheese – grated cheddar or gruyere | $1\frac{1}{4}$ cups | 113 grams |
| 4 ozs flour | 1 scant cup | 113 grams |
| $\frac{1}{2}$ oz gelatine | 1 tablespoon | 14 grams |
| 4 ozs golden syrup | $\frac{1}{4}$ scant cup | 113 grams |
| 4 ozs raisins, sultanas | $\frac{1}{2}$ cup | 113 grams |
| 8 ozs rice | 1 cup | 227 grams |
| 8 ozs sugar – demerara | $1\frac{1}{4}$ cups | 227 grams |
| 8 ozs sugar – castor | 1 cup | 227 grams |
| 1 pint | $2\frac{1}{2}$ cups | $\frac{4}{7}$ litre |
| $1\frac{3}{4}$ pints | $4\frac{3}{8}$ cups | 1 litre |
| 1 pound | 1 pound | 453.56 grams |

The spoon quantities in this book are based on plastic measuring spoons. Level spoons have been used throughout unless otherwise stated.

# Oven Temperature Chart

| Thermostat Settings | Electrical Settings | Heat of Oven |
|---|---|---|
| $\frac{1}{4}$ | 225° | very cool |
| $\frac{1}{2}$ | 250° | very cool |
| 1 | 275° | very cool |
| 2 | 300° | cool |
| 3 | 325° | warm |
| 4 | 350° | moderate |
| 5 | 375° | fairly hot |
| 6 | 400° | fairly hot |
| 7 | 425° | hot |
| 8 | 450° | very hot |
| 9 | 475° | very hot |

Reproduced with permission from the Gas Council.

# Culinary Terms

**Barding** covering meat, poultry or game, with a slice of pork fat to protect the meat, and keep it juicy.

**Basting** spooning hot fat over food that is roasting, to prevent it from drying.

**Beurre-manié** see page 133.

**Blanching** cooking in boiling water as a preliminary process, usually just for a few minutes; another form of blanching is when boiling water is poured over almonds and tomatoes etc. to loosen their skins.

**Blending** combining ingredients slowly and carefully together, by stirring all the time to keep the mixture smooth and creamy.

**Blood temperature** 98.4°F.

**Bouquet garni** bunch of herbs; wrap a bay leaf, a sprig of thyme, and 2 or 3 parsley stalks, in a piece of butter muslin and tie with a thick thread.

**Burnt nuts** nuts which have been fried gently in a little butter until they are dark brown; in the case of almonds it is necessary to blanch them first to remove their skins.

**Creaming** beating butter, or a mixture of butter and sugar together, with a fork until it becomes light and fluffy.

**Kneading** working with the knuckles, using gentle pressure.

**Marinade** used to tenderize and flavour meat or game before cooking; usually made with a mixture of herbs, oil and wine or vinegar.

**Pound** to crush by using pressure; the best results are achieved with a pestle and mortar.

**Roux** a base for sauces and soups; flour and fat are cooked together to form a roux before any liquid is added

**Reducing** boiling quickly to lose some of the liquid; this will not only thicken the stock, but give it a more concentrated flavour.

**Sauté** to fry slowly in a little fat or oil.

**Scalding temperature** a heat just below simmering point, 170°–180°F.

**Seasoned flour** flour to which salt and pepper have been added.

**Shred** to cut in long thin strips.

**Simmering** heating liquid to a temperature where slight movement can just be seen, 180°–190°F.

**Stock** is made from meat or poultry bones cooked in liquid with onion and seasoning and often other vegetables; at the end of the cooking time the liquid is strained. Fish bones can also be used for stock.

**Zest** the outer, coloured skin, of an orange or lemon.

# Index

| | | | | |
|---|---|---|---|---|
| Culinary Terms | 140 | Miscellaneous | 132 |
| Dinner Party Menus | 8 | Oven Temperature Chart | 139 |
| Fork Supper Party Menus | 68 | Sauces | 122 |
| Ideas for Drinks Parties | 98 | Store Cupboard | 88 |
| Lunch Party Menus | 42 | Unexpected Guest, The | 86 |
| Measurement Equivalents | 139 | Vegetables | 109 |

Individual Dishes are listed on the following pages in alphabetical order under the headings First Courses, Main Courses, Puddings etc.

## Drinks Parties

| | | | |
|---|---|---|---|
| Artichoke Leaves with Prawns | 101 | Mushroom & Shrimp Vol-au-Vent | 105 |
| Celery, Stuffed* | 108 | NUTS | |
| Chicken Liver Pâté, Quick* | 101 | Devilled Peanuts* | 103 |
| Dates and Grapes, Stuffed | 104 | Salted Almond Sandwiches | 103 |
| DIPS | | Nut Cheese Balls | 103 |
| Avocado Dip* | 100 | Onion Puffs | 102 |
| Cauliflower Dip | 100 | Pastry Petits Fours | 104 |
| Tuna Fish Dip* | 100 | Prune and Bacon Rolls | 107 |
| Double-Decker Sandwiches | 102 | Sausage Balls | 106 |
| Ham and Asparagus Squares | 105 | Sausage Pastry Rings | 106 |
| Kidney and Bacon Rolls | 107 | | |

## First Courses

| | | | |
|---|---|---|---|
| Barbecue Ribs with Sweet Spiced Sauce | 32 | FISH | |
| | | Buckling with Cheese and Tomatoes* | 62 |
| Cold Consommé with Mock Caviar and Soured Cream* | 36 | Cod with Crab Sauce Mornay | 30 |
| | | Cold Mackerel with Mayonnaise | 26 |
| Consommé with Egg and Parmesan Cheese | 89 | Crab Mousse | 22 |
| | | Herrings in Soured Cream* | 90 |
| Consommé Mousse | 40 | Mussels with Garlic Breadcrumbs | 16 |
| EGGS | | Salmon Mould | 70 |
| Eggs Benedict | 94 | Smoked Cod Mousse | 82 |
| Egg Mousse | 24 | Squid Vinaigrette | 58 |
| Oeufs en Cocotte* | 52 | Steamed Fish Soufflé | 60 |
| Soufflé Oeuf en Cocotte | 89 | Taramasalata | 66 & 89* |

Recipes marked with an asterisk are quick to prepare; those in italics require no cooking

# Index

PÂTÉS

| | | | |
|---|---|---|---|
| *Buckling Pâté* | 38 | Watercress Soup, Cream of | 14 |
| Chicken Liver Pâté* | 76 | FRUIT AND VEGETABLES | |
| Egg and Liver Pâté* | 10 | *Apple, Celery and Prawn Cocktail* | 46 |
| Chicken Liver Pâté,* Quick | 101 | Artichokes with Garlic Breadcrumbs | 20 |
| *Fish Pâté* | 28 | *Avocado Cream with Prawns* | 50 |
| Kipper Pâté* | 34 | Avocado Pear with Crab Meat, Baked | 18 |
| Pâté Maison | 84 | Aubergines with Cheese, Baked | 116 |
| SOUPS | | *Fennel, Spinach and Avocado Pear* | |
| Artichoke Soup, Thick | 78 | *Salad* | 111 |
| *Gazpacho* | 80 | *Grapefruit and Prawn Cocktail* | 48 |
| Onion Soup | 72 | Grapefruit with Brown Sugar, Hot* | 44 |
| Mock Bisque* | 90 | Ratatouille | 113 |
| Mushroom Soup, Quick* | 64 | Salad Niçoise | 54 |
| Squid Soup | 12 | *Stuffed Tomatoes* | 56 |
| Vichyssoise | 74 | | |

## Main Courses

| | | | |
|---|---|---|---|
| BACON AND HAM | | Steamed Fish Souffle* | 60 |
| Baked Gammon with Prunes and | | FLANS | |
| Apricots | 22 | Egg and Bacon Pie* | 94 |
| Boiled Bacon with Sweet Cider Sauce* | 54 | Quiche Lorraine* | 58 |
| Ham and Pimento Kebabs* | 92 | GAME | |
| BEEF | | Jugged Hare | 14 |
| Bœuf en Croûte* | 38 | Pheasant, Roast, with Raisins and | |
| Cabbage Rolls, Stuffed, in Tomato | | Whisky | 12 |
| Sauce | 74 | Pigeon Casserole* | 26 |
| Chilli Con Carne* | 95 | Rabbit with Prunes and Apples* | 50 |
| Curried Beef | 78 | LAMB | |
| Goulash* | 60 | Lamb Chops en Croûte | 62 |
| Meat Loaf | 70 | Moussaka | 48 |
| Peppers, Stuffed | 32 | Shoulder of Lamb, Braised, with | |
| Roast, Cold, with Soured Cream, | | Ratatouille | 44 |
| Olives and Lemon Slices | 72 | Shoulder of Lamb, Stuffed | 16 |
| Steak and Kidney Pudding | 52 | OFFAL | |
| EGGS | | Kidney Casserole with Sausages* | 46 |
| Eggs Benedict* | 94 | PASTA AND RICE | |
| Omelette Arnold Bennett* | 91 | Chinese Risotto | 93 |
| FISH | | Lasagne* | 93 |
| Cod Coulibiac | 10 | Tuna Fish Cannelloni* | 92 |
| Fish Pie | 56 | PORK AND VEAL | |
| Kedgeree* | 91 | Blanquette de Veau | 76 |

Recipes marked with an asterisk are quick to prepare; those in italics require no cooking

# Index

| | |
|---|---|
| Courgettes, Aubergines and | |
| Tomatoes, Stuffed | 34 |
| Paupiettes de Porc | 24 |
| Pork Chops with Anchovies* | 30 |
| Terrine of Pork | 82 |
| Vitello Tonnato* | 20 |
| POULTRY | |
| Chicken and Almonds in Lemon | |
| Sauce | 84 |

| | |
|---|---|
| Chicken Curry, Mild | 66 |
| Fried Chicken* | 36 |
| Chicken and Ham Mousse | 64 |
| Cold Chicken in Mild Curry Sauce | 80 |
| Coq au Vin | 18 |
| Duck Casserole with Oranges and | |
| Cider | 28 |
| Turkey, Roast | 40 |

## Puddings

| | |
|---|---|
| Apples with Ground Almonds | 96 |
| Batter Pudding | 50 |
| Biscuit Flan | 46 |
| Brandy Snaps | 20 |
| Caramel Custard with Raisins | 64 |
| Caramel Oranges | 38 |
| Christmas Pudding | 40 |
| Chocolate Cherry Gâteau | 80 |
| Chocolate Meringue Crumble | 74 |
| Chocolate Pots* | 28 |
| Coffee Meringue Flan | 58 |
| Crème Brûlée | 14 |
| Crème de Menthe Jelly | 70 |
| Damsons with Baked Bread | 96 |
| French Apple Flan | 60 |
| Fresh Fruit Salad | 76 |
| Gâteau avec Crème au Chocolat | 44 |
| Ginger Cream* | 10 |
| Ginger Cream Log* | 32 |
| Ginger Pudding | 56 |
| Lemon Soufflé | 72 |
| Lemon Syllabub* | 62 |
| Lemon Meringues | 22 |
| Lychee and Black Grape Salad | 84 |

| | |
|---|---|
| ICE-CREAM | |
| Blackcurrant Ice-cream | 30 |
| Mousse d'Amandes au Caramel | |
| Glacée | 12 |
| Vanilla Ice-cream with Chocolate | |
| Sauce | 16 |
| Madame Pusich's Iced Pineapple | |
| Gâteau | 82 |
| Marmalade Curd | 66 |
| Marsala Cream* | 48 |
| Melon Baskets | 24 |
| Oeufs à la Neige | 26 |
| Orange Cream Soufflé Surprise | 18 |
| Pancakes | 96 |
| Peaches with Cream and Caramel | 78 |
| Pears with Chocolate Sauce* | 97 |
| Pear and Grape Compôte | 52 |
| Profiteroles au Chocolat | 32 |
| Raisins avec Crème Chantilly | 34 |
| Summer Pudding | 54 |
| Summer Pudding, Hatch House | 36 |
| Queen's Peaches* | 95 |
| Zabaione | 97 |

## Vegetables

| | |
|---|---|
| Aubergines, Baked, with Cheese | 116 |
| Beetroot with Grapes | 116 |
| Carrots, Baked | 118 |
| Celery, Braised | 115 |
| Chicory, Braised | 115 |

| | |
|---|---|
| Chou aux Pommes | 117 |
| Courgettes | 117 |
| POTATOES | |
| Baked Potatoes | 119 |
| Potato Casserole | 119 |

Recipes marked with an asterisk are quick to prepare; those in italics require no cooking

143

| | | | |
|---|---|---|---|
| Potato Crust | 118 | *Fennel, Spinach and Avocado Pear* | |
| Ratatouille | 113 | *Salad** | 111 |
| Red Cabbage | 114 | *Green Salad* | 111 |
| RICE | | Rice Salad | 112 |
| Boiled Rice | 120 | Tomato Chartreuse | 113 |
| Rice for Curry | 121 | *Tomato Salad* | 112 |
| Rice Pilaff | 121 | Winter Salad | 112 |
| Spiced Rice | 120 | Spinach, Creamed | 117 |
| SALADS | | Vegetable Marrow Italian Style | 114 |
| *Apple, Celery and Walnut Salad* | 111 | | |

## Sauces

| | | | |
|---|---|---|---|
| BASIC AND SAVOURY | | Tomato Sauce I | 125 |
| *Aïoli Sauce* | 129 | Tomato Sauce II | 126 |
| Béchamel Sauce | 123 | *Vinaigrette Sauce** | 128 |
| Beurre Manié | 133 | White Sauce | 123 |
| Bread Sauce | 126 | White Wine Sauce | 126 |
| Brown Sauce | 124 | SWEET SAUCES | |
| Espagnole Sauce | 124 | *Brandy Butter* | 131 |
| Gravy, Simple* | 125 | Chocolate Cream | 130 |
| Hollandaise, Blender* | 128 | Chocolate Sauce I | 129 |
| *Mayonnaise, Egg* | 127 | Chocolate Sauce II* | 130 |
| *Mayonnaise, Blender** | 127 | Custard Sauce | 129 |

## Miscellaneous

| | | | |
|---|---|---|---|
| Batter | 136 | Chestnut Stuffing | 137 |
| Beurre Manié | 133 | Forcemeat | 136 |
| BREAD | | Macaroons | 135 |
| Breadcrumbs, Fried | 135 | PASTRY | |
| Croûtons | 135 | Puff Pastry | 133 |
| Garlic Bread | 134 | Short Crust Pastry | 133 |
| Melba Toast | 134 | Poached Eggs | 138 |
| Chicken, Boiled | 137 | Poppadums | 136 |

Recipes marked with an asterisk are quick to prepare; those in italics require no cooking